The Somerset & Dorset Files

No.6

A Railway Bylines Special
By Martin Smith

High Street, Shepton Mallet, undated postcard.

IRWELL PRESS Ltd.

Copyright IRWELL PRESS LIMITED
ISBN-978-1-906919-01-6
First published in the United
Kingdom in 2008
by Irwell Press Limited, 59A, High
Street, Clophill,
Bedfordshire MK45 4BE
Printed by Newnorth Print, Bedford
Tel: 01525 861888
Fax: 01525 862044
www.irwellpress.co.uk

Veteran 3F 43734 has arrived at Burnham-on-Sea with the 1.20pm ex-Evercreech Junction on 20 August 1960. Although this train was advertised to terminate at Highbridge, on Wednesdays and Saturdays it continued unadvertised to Burnham. *Photograph: Leslie Freeman; www.transporttreasury.co.uk*

Cover photograph: 'Jinty' 47557 returns light to Radstock after banking a Down train up to Masbury on 6 July 1959. *Photograph: R.C.Riley; www.transporttreasury.co.uk*

Acknowledgements

During the preparation of this book, reference was made to S&D, LMS, British Railways and Board of Trade minute books and documents. Reference was also made to *The Somerset & Dorset Railway* by Robin Atthill (David & Charles, 1967), *Radstock – Coal and Steam* by Chris Handley (Millstream Books, 1991) and to various issues of *Five Arches* (the history journal of the Radstock, Midsomer Norton & District Museum Trust; extracts used in this book have been reproduced with the Society's kind permission), *The Pines Express* (the magazine of the S&D Trust), and various contemporary railway periodicals, especially the *Railway Observer*. Thanks to the late Mr. Bryan L.Wilson and Mr. Eric Youldon for invaluable advice and assistance. Thanks also to the late Mr. Geoff Creese, Ms. Julie Dexter (editor, *Five Arches*), Mr. Michael Wyatt and to the photographers and archivists who made their photographs available for publication.
Martin Smith, Coleford, Somerset; October 2008

Bath

A 7F 2-8-0 at Green Park station – what could possibly be more 'S&D' than that? The loco is 53804, but the train is not an ordinary S&D working; it is the Stephenson Locomotive Society's special to Templecombe and back, which ran on Sunday 11 September 1960. The train was advertised to leave Bath 'shortly after 2pm' and arrive back 'in time for half-day excursions to London, Birmingham etc'. The cost of the trip was 10/-. The participants had a little time to themselves at Templecombe while 53804 went to Evercreech Junction to be turned for the return trip; although there was a turntable at Templecombe shed it could not accommodate a 7F. One of the many items of interest in this picture is the shed behind 53804 – it is part of H.M.Customs bonded warehouse. The main part of the warehouse was below the station, underground cellars extending the full length of the platforms. Wines and spirits were kept in the cellars, and any railway vans collecting

or delivering these goods had to be loaded/unloaded behind locked doors in the shed in our picture. The subterranean part of the bonded warehouse remained in use until 1967 but the loading shed was not demolished until 1981. As for the station itself, it closed with the S&D on 7 March 1966. Passenger services on the ex-Midland Railway Bristol-Bath branch were also withdrawn on that same day. In 1971 the station was given the status of a listed building and the premises were subsequently acquired by Sainsbury's, the station itself being earmarked for use as a covered car park for their proposed supermarket. By that time the structure had fallen into disrepair, but restoration work started in 1979 and, three years and £1,500,000 later, the superbly restored building – complete with a fully glazed roof once again – was reopened by HRH Princess Margaret on 1 December 1982. In so doing, she probably became the first member of the Royal Family to open a

supermarket car park. The supermarket is still there – it is actually a few yards beyond the west end of the station buildings – but the car park has been moved out from under the roof. Several of the station buildings alongside the platforms are now small shops – there are gift shops, a craft shop and an antiques shop – while, on Mondays-Saturdays, the rest of the space is now used for a covered market. (Saturday is farmers' market day – well worth a visit.) Interestingly, a few community organisations now have offices beneath the station in what was once the bonded warehouse. As a tribute to the site's heritage, three of the approach roads to the supermarket and adjacent retail park were named Ivo Peters Road (after the S&D's best-known photographer), Pines Way (after the Pines Express, of course) and Stanier Road. *Photograph: Hugh Ballantyne*

Looking across the line to Green Park sheds, 22 July 1958. From left to right we have 7F 53800, a 4F 0-6-0 on the coal stage, a 2P 4-4-0 (possibly 40564), a Class 4 2-6-0 (it looks like 73116) and a 'Black Five'. The canopy of Green Park station is just about discernible beyond and behind the stone-built former Midland shed. *Photograph: R.C.Riley; www.transporttreasury.co.uk*

Class 4 2-6-0 76025 bursts out of the northern end of Combe Down Tunnel. The train has less than half a mile of daylight before plunging into Devonshire Tunnel. This picturesque spot between the two tunnels – Lyncombe Vale – is less than ¾-mile from the centre of Bath as the crow flies. The mouths of the two tunnels are now sealed, but the short stretch of trackbed between the two tunnels, although rather overgrown, can be walked, its official status being that of a 'permissive recreational path'. *Photograph: George Heiron; www.transporttreasury.co.uk*

Class 4 80067 of Templecombe shed diverges on to the S&D line at Bath Junction and starts the 1 in 50 slog up to Devonshire Tunnel with a three-coach local in May 1965. The signal is a typical Midland Railway item. *Photograph: Peter Barnfield*

Right. Standard Class 4 2-6-4T 80057 arrives at Midford with the 3.20pm Bath-Templecombe on 12 August 1965. Whereas we are looking at glorious sunshine seen in this picture, anyone who had been working on the S&D in early December 1960 would have remembered a very different scenario. Incessant rain throughout 3 and 4 December of that year brought considerable disruption throughout the south-west, and on the S&D it caused a land slip near Midford. The line had to be closed to through traffic. Many of the train services started and terminated at Radstock, buses being laid on to take passengers between there and Bath, but the northbound 'Pines Express' was diverted via Fordingbridge, Salisbury, Westbury, Bath Spa and Bristol Stapleton Road, then on to Westerleigh where it picked up the Midland line. These arrangements continued until the S&D was reopened on 10 December. *Photograph: Eric Ashton Collection*

Below. And here's what the station looked like without a train on 29 September 1962. Some years after the closure of the S&D there were thoughts of establishing a preservation site at Midford and turning the station into a museum. The vegetation was cleared, and in 1986 a length of 2-foot gauge track was laid and two small diesel locomotives were acquired. But that was as far as things went. Local residents, fearing that the railway and museum would bring additional traffic to the narrow roads in the area, objected to the scheme and the project ground to a halt after less than a year. A separate plan by the landlord of the neighbouring Hope & Anchor pub to extend the pub car park over the disused viaduct also fell by the wayside; however, attitudes eventually changed – at least in part – and, twenty years on, the pub car park now extends across the trackbed at the south end of the station. *Photograph: Peter Barnfield*

Bottom right. 2P 4-4-0 40698 crosses Midford Viaduct with a northbound local on 6 July 1959. The photographer is standing on the trackbed of the old GWR branch between Limpley Stoke and Hallatrow – this is, of course, the very line which was used during the filming of *The Titfield Thunderbolt*. The Limpley Stoke-Hallatrow line did not reach Midford until 1910 but, the previous year, the S&D Joint Committee had proposed a connection with the as-yet-unfinished GWR line at Midford. The estimated cost of the connection was £30,000, but the S&D was prepared to make that outlay only if the owners of collieries at Camerton and Dunkerton (four miles or so to the west) would guarantee a specified amount of traffic for a specified number of years. The colliery owners could not or would not give such a guarantee, so the connection was not built. As things turned out, the collieries in question did not have particularly lengthy lives. Dunkerton closed in 1927; in its short working life of around twenty years it had been the most productive in North Somerset – at its peak it raised more than 150,000 tons per annum – but it had also had by far the worst history of labour relations of any of the North Somerset pits. In 1946 it was proposed to reopen Dunkerton and connect it to Camerton Colliery, but that scheme did not come to fruition. Camerton itself remained in production only until April 1950. It had latterly been virtually the sole *raison d'être* for the GWR's branch from Limpley Stoke, and the last section of the branch closed completely the following February. *Photograph: R.C.Riley; www.transporttreasury.co.uk*

Radstock shed

Although shunting and banking engines were stationed at Radstock from an early date, it seems that they were stabled in the open as there was no engine shed until the 1890s. The original shed was a small single-road building which was constructed circa 1895/96, but it seems that there was a lack of foresight as, in 1898, plans were announced for a new shed. The new building – a two-road structure – was built on the same site and was completed in 1901. It is this shed which survived until – and, indeed, for some years after – the end of the S&D. Here, 'Jinty' 47275 trundles back alongside the shed on 12 July 1960. The shed spent its life as a sub-shed of Bath which, in late LMS days, was coded 22C. After being transferred to the Southern Region in 1950 it became 71G, and on transfer to the Western Region in 1958 it became 82F. *Photograph: R.C.Riley; www.transporttreasury.co.uk*

Left. 'Turn sharp right outside Radstock North station along a road running parallel to the line. Turn right into a rough road leading over the line and a path leads to the shed from the right-hand side. Walking time 5 minutes.' Those directions from Flt.Lt.Aidan Fuller's fabled *Locoshed Directory* got one to Radstock engine shed. The shed was tucked away behind sidings on the south side of the running lines to the east of the station. Said building is in the mid-distance of this picture. As a reminder that Radstock was an important centre of the mining industry, the train on the left (an Up train hauled by a 7F 2-8-0 – it could be 53806) is loaded with what appears to be very fine coal – possibly 'duff' for a power station – while, in the sidings on the right, apart from a few vans and one wagon loaded with what looks like scrap timber, almost everything on view is colliery-related. The picture was taken in October 1956. *Photograph: Derek Clayton*

Below. Coaling at Radstock was undertaken by means of small tubs which were hoisted up by a crane and tipped into the locomotive's bunker below. It was a primitive method but, as we have seen in other books in this series, the very same method was used at Templecombe and Highbridge. In this picture, 47557 is being coaled on 5 September 1963. For the last thirty or so years of the shed's life, the mainstay of its fleet were 'Jintys'. They were used on local shunting and, importantly, also for banking goods trains on the main line. Evidence of the banking duties is revealed by the uncoupling hook dangling from 47557's smokebox handrail – these hooks were used to uncouple banking engines from the rear of trains at Masbury. A visitor to Radstock on 11 September 1960 reported that 47275, 47316, 47496 and 47557 were on shed. It was noted that one of the local 'Jintys' had recently been used at Radstock Wagon Works while Sentinel 47190 had been away. A further visitor on the afternoon of 10 August 1965 found that 47506 was the only occupant of Radstock shed '...but 47554 arrived light engine from the Bath direction and went on shed'. One of the Radstock 'Jintys' – and one of their brethren at Bath – had had a moment of glory on Christmas Eve 1959. A Bournemouth-Sheffield relief unexpectedly required assistance at Evercreech Junction and took the only available pilot loco, so as the next northbound train – the 'Pines Express', headed by Bulleid Pacific 34028 *Eddystone* - would be calling there to pick up a pilot, and as there were no pilots left there, a desperate call was sent out to Radstock. All they could come up with was a 'Jinty', which was duly dispatched to Evercreech and helped the 'Pines' up to Masbury. It was considered unwise for the 'Jinty' to remain at the front of the train for the descent over the Mendips, so it was taken off at Binegar. However, the Pacific's crew reckoned that it would be foolhardy to do the climb through Combe Down Tunnel at Bath unaided, so another Jinty – 47496 – was sent out from Bath to wait at Midford, where it was attached to the front of the train and helped it to Bath. *Photograph: David Idle; www.transporttreasury.co.uk*

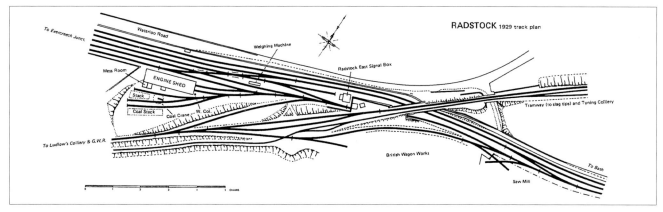

RADSTOCK 1929 track plan

Top left. 47496 stands alongside the water columns at Radstock shed on 18 August 1962. Although Radstock shed officially closed with the S&D in March 1966, it continued to be used as a stabling point for a diesel shunter which was used for the coal traffic from Writhlington Colliery. In 1969 the shed was acquired by the Somerset & Dorset Circle (the forerunner of today's S&D Trust) and became home to a number of items of preserved rolling stock, including 7F 2-8-0 53808. During the next few years there were several 'steam' days, mainly with former industrial tank engines which had also been saved for preservation. However, all that came to an end in 1975. British Railways had quoted a price of £54,000 (plus the inevitable VAT) for the purchase of the land and track, and that was beyond the budget of the preservationists. The stock was moved away. Rather appropriately, the last locomotive to go was 53808 which, by that time, was in the throes of being restored as S&D No.88. It was taken out by a 'Class 33' diesel on 16 October 1975; this was the last ever rail movement over the two level crossings in the centre of Radstock. The S&D Trust later set up home at Washford on the West Somerset Railway, and the beautifully restored Prussian Blue No.88 is now one of the main attractions on the WSR itself. *Photograph: Paul Cottrell*

Bottom left. Radstock's two Sentinel shunters, 47190 and 47191, stand outside the shed on 22 July 1958. The S&D Joint Committee took delivery of the two Sentinels in 1929 to replace the antiquated 'Dazzlers', the small shunting engines which had previously been used at Radstock. The S&D's minute books record that the Sentinels were originally intended '…for use on the Ludlows, Writhlington and Clandown branches', but that told only part of the story. With their low cab roofs and dropped footplates, the Sentinels were one of the very few types which could pass under the severely limited clearance of 'Marble Arch', the bridge which carried the Tyning Colliery tramway across part of the S&D yard at Radstock. The distinctive shape of Sentinel locomotives was because they had vertical boilers and vertically mounted cylinders. The boiler was in the front part of the cab – the rim of the chimney can just about be seen in this picture. This particular type of Sentinel had two pairs of cylinders; they were positioned behind the two hinged flaps on the side of the bodywork (the flaps giving access for

maintenance). The drive to the front axle was by means of a chain, the axles themselves being coupled by another chain. Sentinel locomotives were a little more expensive to buy than conventional locomotives – in 1927 a 'mid range' sentinel cost £1,600 whereas a typical industrial-type 0-4-0 tank locomotive cost around £1,000-£1,200 – but they offered significant savings in the long term. Compared to a conventional locomotive, a Sentinel could haul 25% more weight, consumed less than half the coal and water, and cost less than half for repairs and maintenance. Furthermore, Sentinels could be operated by one man. No fewer than 305 Sentinel steam locomotives of various types were built for customers in the United Kingdom between 1923 and 1958. The majority went to industrial users; only 68 went to 'main line' railway companies – 58 to the LNER, 6 to the LMS, 2 to the GWR and, of course, two to the S&D. The S&D's Sentinels were originally S&D 101 and 102 but, after the LMS took over responsibility for S&D locomotive matters in 1930 they became LMS 7190 and 7191. Under BR auspices they duly became 47190 and 47191. Somewhat perversely, each of the two Sentinels was occasionally found work on other parts of the LMS system, and this meant that a suitably small locomotive had to be drafted to Radstock to deputise. Between 1931 and 1952 the role of deputy fell to ex-Lancashire & Yorkshire 0-4-0ST 11202 (later BR 51202), which spent long periods at Radstock. Nevertheless, both of the Sentinels eventually returned to Radstock and they were to see out their days there. 47191 was withdrawn in August 1959. 47190 went in March 1961, the demolition of 'Marble Arch' the previous year having brought to an end the need for 'low height' shunters in the town. It is thought that 47190 had been steamed only once since the previous summer, and that was down to an emergency. To explain… During the torrential rain which hit the area on 3 and 4 December 1960 part of the railway at Radstock was flooded so, as a precaution in case the shed had to be evacuated, all the locos were steamed. This was believed to have been the first time 47190 had been steamed for about six months. To the surprise of many, it was subsequently used for a little light shunting work but, after that unaccustomed exertion, it went into retirement again and, as far as can be determined, never again turned a wheel in anger. Before leaving Radstock for the last time in this series of books, let it not be thought that the town's industrial heritage has left a visual blight. No, sir! The area has great character and, by way of a testament, a number of well-known people have chosen to live here. And when it comes to well-known people – the rich and famous – you can't get much more rich or famous than Hollywood megastar Johnny Depp, who lives near Timsbury. This writer has bumped into him at Tescos in Paulton. Name-dropping? Who, me? *Photograph: R.C.Riley; www.transporttreasury.co.uk*

Midsomer Norton

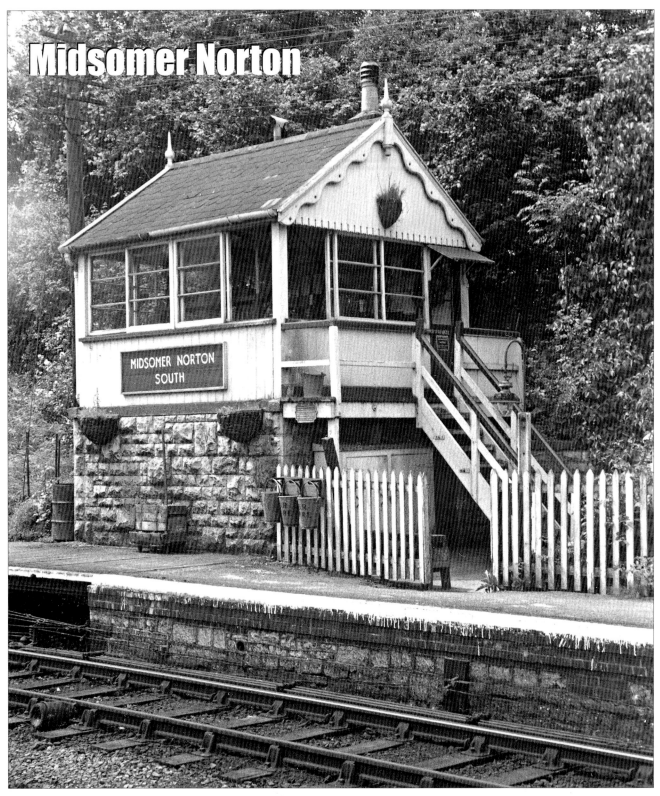

And here's one for the modellers... The handsome signal box on the Up platform at Midsomer Norton station confirms that, by the time this picture was taken in 1964, the establishment's full title was Midsomer Norton South. The 'South' suffix had been added in September 1950 in order to differentiate it from Midsomer Norton & Welton station on the ex-GWR Bristol-Radstock-Frome branch. However, that had not been the station's first name change. Having opened as Midsomer Norton in 1898, it had been renamed Midsomer Norton & Welton (yes – the very name adopted by BR for the 'other' station in 1949), and in September 1949 it had become Midsomer Norton Upper. So the addition of the 'South' suffix in 1950 brought about its fourth title. The desire to differentiate between the S&D and GWR stations for administrative purposes was understandable, but from the locals' point of view it all seemed rather unnecessary as the two stations were

hardly in close proximity – the GWR station on the Bristol-Frome line was in the 'suburb' of Welton, the best part of a mile to the north. These days, visitors to the area often ask whether Midsomer Norton is the 'Midsomer' of the TV series Midsomer Murders. It is not. To the best of our knowledge the TV series is filmed in Buckinghamshire. The nearest Midsomer Norton gets to mass bloodshed these days are the regular visits of the 'Give a Pint of Blood' people to the Somer Centre in Gullock Tyning off Rackvernal Road. The hall, incidentally, is adjacent to the old S&D trackbed near Norton Hill Colliery, so after giving a pinta one can have a reviving stroll along the old line. (On a serious note... If you're not already a blood donor, please DO enrol. If YOU ever needed blood in an emergency, you'd expect it to be immediately available – and that works both ways. Dismounts from soapbox...). *Photograph: Peter Barnfield*

To Masbury

Northbound trains had an 8½-mile climb up to Masbury Summit, though this was not unbroken as there was a brief section of downhill at Shepton Mallet. Nevertheless, much of the 8½ miles was at 1 in 50. Here, Class 4 2-6-0 76015 and Bulleid Pacific 34043 *Combe Martin* have made it up the gradient and are broaching the summit with the 10.05am Bournemouth West-Bradford on 1 September 1962. The leading coaches are Gresley articulated stock. The bridge in the distance takes the B3135 road to Cheddar over the railway. *Photograph: Hugh Ballantyne*

7F 2-8-0 53801 heads an Up local near Masbury Summit on 18 July 1959. The four-coach set (No.390) was one of eight Maunsell sets on the S&D. Going back many, many years, E.L.Ahrons had memories of Masbury. He recalled that, in the 1870s, '…the old dark-green engines were not much to look at, as far as appearance and somewhat diminutive size went, but when it came to running down banks of 1 in 50 at high speeds they were all there. As they could do little more than crawl up one side of the bank, the drivers made amends by letting the engines out for all they were worth down the other side. Further, since the trains consisted of four-wheeled coaches, the age of which was extremely uncertain, the side-to-side motion was somewhat appalling, especially between Binegar and Evercreech Junction, where I more than once thought that my days were about to end'. *Photograph: R.C.Riley; www.transporttreasury.co.uk*

Winsor Hill

1½ miles to the south of Masbury halt were Winsor Hill Tunnels. Here, Class 4 2-6-0 76015 has emerged from the north end of the Up line tunnel with the 1.10pm Bournemouth West-Bristol on 3 September 1963; it seems to be coping well with the 1 in 50 gradient. When the line was built in 1874 it had only a single track which passed through a 239-yard bore under Windsor Hill, but when the line was doubled in 1892 a separate tunnel, 126 yards in length, was bored on the west side of the original one. In his 'standard' history of the line, author Robin Atthill tells us that, during the construction fo the original tunnel, four navvies were killed by a rockfall on 18 Augusat 1873. They were buried in the cemetary at Shepton Mallet under a monument fashioned from a portion of the rock which cause their deaths. The inscription on the stone reads 'For man also knoweth not his time'. It might have been noticed that the foregoing refers to Winsor Hill Tunnels (Winsor without

a 'd') and to them passing under Windsor Hill (Windsor with a 'd'). The hill itself appears on Ordnance Survey maps as Windsor Hill, but the location and the nearby quarry appear on railway maps as Winsor Hill. Yer takes yer money… An interesting aspect of this picture is the rusted and partly overgrown rails in the foreground. These were part of set of sidings – Hamwood Sidings – which had been used by traffic from Hamwood Quarry. The sidings were not lifted until the early 1960s but this photograph confirms that they had not been used for some considerable time beforehand. Hamwood Quarry itself was about ¼-mile to the west of the railway, a non-locomotive 2ft gauge tramway and incline being used to bring the stone down to the sidings alongside the S&D. On the opposite side of the line there had at one time been another set of sidings serving Winsor Hill Quarry. These were installed in 1875 and were removed in 1957. The building next to

the last coach of the train is the old signal box between the two tracks; the 'box opened in 1892 when the line was doubled and was last used in 1948. *Photograph: David Idle; www.transporttreasury.co.uk*

In this view of the south end of Winsor Hill Tunnels the two separate bores can be clearly seen. Class 4 4-6-0 75071 has emerged from the original 239-yard bore and continues down the 1 in 50 with the 3.20pm Bath-Templecombe on 5 September 1963. Just out of view behind the photographer's right shoulder is the formation of a siding which served Downside Quarry, to the east of the railway. The siding had opened in 1900 but had been taken out of use in 1940. The catch points on the Up line on the left were intended to derail any vehicles which had broken away and run back on the 1 in 50. *Photograph: David Idle; www.transporttreasury.co.uk*

Working of stone sidings, Winsor Hill:—

The following regulations as to working these sidings must be carried out by the guard or shunter in charge of the stone train working between Shepton Mallet and Winsor Hill:—

Loaded wagons must be taken from the sidings by an engine working to Shepton Mallet, and the driver and guard must take care that sufficient wagon brakes are pinned down to ensure complete control of the train between Winsor Hill and Shepton Mallet. Load not to exceed 20 wagons.

When working empty wagons from Shepton Mallet to Mendip Siding at Winsor Hill, the train must be drawn clear of the crossover road points, and the guard must thoroughly secure it by putting on the van brake and making use of sprags and wagon brakes as may be necessary in addition. The engine must then be uncoupled from the train, and must run forward to Masbury, cross over at that station, and return to Winsor Hill on the proper line, and then perform the shunting necessary for placing the wagons in the siding.

Up banked freight trains may, when instructions are given for this to be done, take wagons to Mendip Siding at Winsor Hill. Wagons for Mendip Siding must be placed between the last brake van of the train and the banking engine, and when the train has come to a stand clear of the crossover road, the guard in charge must, after securing his own train, uncouple the wagons from his rear brake van, and these must then be shunted into the siding by the banking engine.

Loaded wagons must not be left on the down main line attached to the brake van whilst the engine is in the sidings. A guard's van, only if absolutely necessary, may be left on the main line with brake well secured whilst the engine draws out the loaded wagons from the siding.

Wagons for Hamwood Quarry Siding must be placed next the train engine.

Winsor Hill—Downside siding:—

A roadway across the rails to the new plant (first inside the gate) in the siding has been constructed.

Special care must be exercised by the guard or shunter in charge to see the line is clear before shunting operations commence.

Engines, on arriving to work this siding, must be brought to a stand with the wagons well clear of the plant and must not again move forward until hand signalled by the man in charge of shunting operations.

This siding will be worked in the same manner as shown in this Appendix for the working of the stone sidings, Winsor Hill, but in addition the guard or shunter will call at the Shepton Mallet signal box for the keys of the Downside sidings ground frame, and on reaching there with his engine or train will unlock the small bell box, fixed at the side of the ground frame, and work the point and signal frame in accordance with the instructions exhibited at the ground frame.

Great care must be taken to see that the guards' vans and wagons (if any) that are left on the main line are fully and properly secured, sprags being used if necessary before the engine is detached to go into the siding.

The empty wagons must be detached on the siding nearest Shepton Mallet, and the loaded wagons taken from the other siding. No shunting must be done in these sidings beyond simply placing the empties on one line, and taking the loaded ones from the other, it being of the utmost importance that the work should be done as quickly as possible to avoid blocking the main line.

The guard or shunter on reaching Shepton Mallet will hand over the keys of the ground frame to the signalman on duty, who will retain them until again required.

Should the appointed trains not be able to clear out all the wagons for Downside siding, such surplus wagons may be placed behind the last brake van of an up single load freight train, with a bank engine at the rear of them. The shunter, before starting from Shepton Mallet, will advise the signalman there what is about to be done and obtain from him the special disc marked "Downside Siding." The train must stop at Winsor Hill signal box clear of the crossover road, and the shunter in charge of the wagons for Downside siding will then uncouple them from the rear brake van of the train (which can then proceed on its journey); he will then place on the draw-bar hook of the last wagon the "Downside siding" disc, and the signalman at Winsor Hill, after obtaining the necessary permission from Shepton Mallet on the block instrument for the engine and wagons to proceed, the wagons will then be placed in the Downside siding in accordance with the regulations as shown above.

After the wagons have been placed in the siding the shunter must take the "Downside siding" disc, with the engine, back to Shepton Mallet, and hand the same over to the signalman on duty, who must not give the "Train out of section" signal to the signalman at Winsor Hill until the disc has been handed over to him.

Shepton Mallet

Left. With 4F 44146 piloting 34102 *Lapford*, the 9.08am Birmingham (New Street)-Bournemouth West approaches Shepton Mallet on 20 August 1960. Passengers who had come all the way from New Street must have found scenes such as this a sheer delight; New Street is one of the most gloomy, soul-less and thoroughly depressing stations in the land, whereas Shepton Mallet could hardly have been in a more open and airy location. (In case born-and-bred Birmingham folk think that I'm taking a swipe at their city – I'm not. I'm taking a swipe at New Street station. Unfortunately, whenever I've had to change trains there I've never had a quick, easy connection – I've always had to endure a lengthy wait which has given me far, far too much time to take it all in.) *Photograph: Leslie Freeman; www.transporttreasury.co.uk*

Bottom left. This picture, which looks southwards through Shepton Mallet station, was taken from the station footbridge on 20 August 1960. The footbridge, which was at the north end of the platforms, was installed in the 1920s to replace the original timber footbridge which was half-way along the platforms (between the shelter and the signal box on the left-hand platform). The general goods yard is at the far end of the station on the right; it had a decent-size goods shed and a 5-ton crane. The sidings behind the Down platform on the left served a stone company and also the Engineer's Department of the railway. The engineers had taken over what used to be the old S&D company's signal works, which had closed in 1930. The presence of a decent range of goods facilities at Shepton Mallet was fitting, as the town was an important one with a long history as a trading centre. Indeed, the history books explained that '…in the reign of Queen Elizabeth (the First) additional impetus was given to the West of England cloth trade by the passing of an Act forbidding the exportation of wool, and Shepton, whose position under the Mendips had made it a prolific wool producing district, became a great cloth manufacturing centre; but the introduction of machinery in the north and its long isolation from railway caused the trade to decline. However, in latter years its trade has revived and velvet and crape (sic) making, brick and pottery works, besides large breweries, and the manufacture of wearing apparel usually purchased in an important agricultural town have made Shepton Mallet a busy place.' *Photograph: Leslie Freeman; www.transporttreasury.co.uk*

Below. A rather different view of Shepton Mallet station, taken on 20 August 1960. This was a peak summer Saturday so, given the total lack of activity at the station – there's not even any anticipation of activity – one assumes that it is fairly late in the day, after the rush has died down. We are looking north. The station approach road from Charlton Road is on the left; in the distance beyond it is a glimpse of Charlton Viaduct. The 'sunken' dead-end line in the foreground is that of the cattle dock; at one time it would have been well used. Parked in the forecourt is a Morris Minor; its registration 36 ENK was issued by Hertfordshire County Council in November 1958. We have a sneaking feeling that it might be the photographer's car. *Photograph: Leslie Freeman; www.transporttreasury.co.uk*

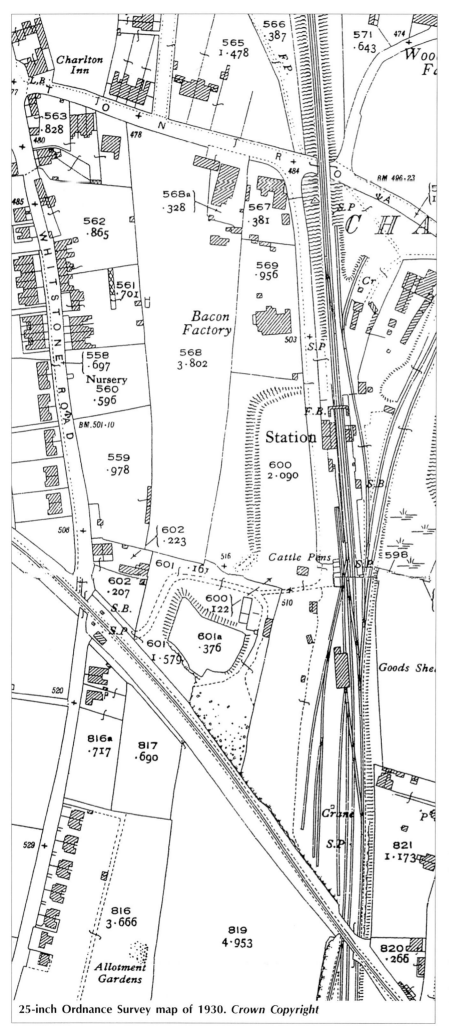

25-inch Ordnance Survey map of 1930. *Crown Copyright*

SHEPTON MALLET
(Som)
Miles 115½. Map Sq. 22.
Pop. 5,131. Clos. day Wed.
HIGH STREET STATION.
From Paddington via Witham.
1st cl.—Single 27/5, Return 54/10.
3rd cl.—Single 18/3, Return 36/6.

Padd. a.m.	Shep.	Shep.	Padd.
5 30s	10 44	9 10r	12 15
10 30	1¶53	p.m.	
		12 1Bsr	5 35
p.m.			
12 30r	3 52	12 45er	5 35
3 30	7¶17	4 4r	7 10
6 0r	9 46	—	—
—	—	—	—
—	—	—	—

No Sunday Trains.

¶ By Slip Carriage to Westbury.
e Not Saturday.
r Refreshment Car.
s Saturday only.

Another Route
CHARLTON ROAD STATION.
From Waterloo via Templecombe.
1st cl.—Single 30/2, Return 60/4.
3rd cl.—Single 20/1, Return 40/2.

W'loo a.m.	Shep.	Shep. a.m.	W'loo
5 40	11 18	7 57r	11 8
9 0r	12 42	10 51r	2 15
11 0r	3 25	p.m.	
p.m.		2 16r	6 33
1 0r	5 1	5 15r	8 25
3 0r	6 11	5 41r	10 8
6 0r	9 32		

No Sunday Trains.

r Refreshment Car.

Buses from Frome Station, every two hours (no service Sunday morning), 44 min. journey.

Above. ABC Railway Guide, March 1956

Top right. Now-preserved 7F 53808 heads away from Shepton Mallet with a southbound coal train circa 1954/55. The train is passing under the ex-GWR Yatton-Cheddar-Wells-Witham branch. *Photograph: D.T.Flook*

Bottom right. 7F 53810 approaches Shepton Mallet with the 1.50pm goods (well – it looks like empties, empties and more empties) from Evercreech Junction to Bath on 6 September 1963. The alignment of the ex-GWR Yatton-Cheddar-Wells-Witham branch can be seen crossing the picture from left to right in the distance. However, appearances are a bit deceptive – the two-arched bridge in the distance is not the one which takes the GWR line over the S&D; the two-arched bridge takes a farm track over the railway – the GWR bridge is obscured by it. Across the fields to the left of and slightly behind the photographer is the hamlet of Cannard's Grave on the Shepton Mallet-Evercreech road (the A361). The name Cannard's Grave is said to date back to the days when a suicide was buried at the nearby crossroads with a stake through his body. One of the two pubs near the crossroads was for many years logically named the Cannards Grave Inn, but in recent years that has been changed to Cannards Well; presumably the more-upbeat name was considered more likely to entice passers-by. (When it comes to doomy-sounding pub names, the Cannards Grave Inn wasn't on its own; we remember finding a Cemetery Inn in Rochdale. There's also a Dublin pub known to all the locals as The Gravediggers; its proper name is Kavanagh's, but its location by Glasnevin Cemetery gave rise to the alternative name. There must be other pubs with similarly macabre or funereal names, but we digress yet again...) *Photograph: R.C.Riley; www.transporttreasury.co.uk*

SHEPTON MALLET.

Instructions to be observed for working all banked trains when passing Shepton Mallet (up line) :—

Train engine drivers, when passing over the summit between the up distant and home signals, must partly close the regulator. When passing the home signal—shut steam off entirely. When passing the up starting signal—put the hand brake on and keep it on until passing the up advanced starting signal; after passing this signal put steam on again.

The driver of the banking engine must keep steam on all the time.

Up banked trains stopping at Shepton Mallet for traffic purposes:—

When it is necessary for up banked trains to stop at Shepton Mallet for the purpose of detaching or attaching, the driver of the banking engine must not respond to the train engine whistle (crow) until he has received the "right away" signal from the guard, who must not give that signal until he is in a position to rejoin the train.

Wainwright & Co.'s stone siding:—

Guards must, when shunting in Wainwright & Co.'s stone tip siding, be careful and see that the trap points are properly set. High-sided vehicles must not be pushed foul of the stone tip near the centre of the dock, and any men engaged in unloading stone from the motor wagons must be warned that shunting operations are about to commence.

Evercreech Junction

Evercreech Junction, 3 September 1960. This view looks southwards; at the far end of the station is the level crossing taking the A371 Shepton Mallet-Castle Cary road over the railway. The dead-end road between the two running lines was used by pilot engines awaiting their next 'assisting' job up the long 1 in 50 climb over the Mendip Hills. The siding was also used as a refuge for Highbridge branch trains; given that Evercreech Junction had only two platform roads, if a Highbridge branch train had a wait between arrival and departure from the Junction it usually moved across to the dead-end siding so as to leave the platform roads free for through trains. That there was space for such a siding between the running lines was a legacy of the railway's origins. The whole of the Somerset Central Railway between Highbridge and Cole was laid with broad gauge (7ft 0½in) rails because the company's trains were originally worked by the Bristol & Exeter Railway which was, of course, a broad gauge concern. To allow for the additional width of the broad gauge, station platforms obviously had to be spaced more widely apart than would be necessary with the standard gauge. When the line was converted to the standard gauge the platforms were not repositioned, so it left a greater than usual gap between the two platforms. In the distance on the opposite side of the level crossing is the distinctive water tower. Since the closure of the railway in 1966 the buildings on the Down platform at Evercreech Junction have been converted into a private residence. The old station forecourt behind these buildings is now part of a small trading estate. The old Railway Hotel adjacent to the level crossing is still there, though after the railway closed it was renamed the Silent Whistle. Some years later it was renamed again, this time as The Natterjack Inn. We're not too sure whether the name has local significance as, to the best of our limited knowledge, the greater proportion of Britain's natterjack toad population is in Cumbria and Scotland, not south Somerset. *Photograph: Leslie Freeman; www.transporttreasury.co.uk*

Right. 4F 0-6-0 44422 crosses the A371 on the approach to Evercreech Junction with a Templecombe-Bath local on 21 September 1963. *Photograph: P.Gomm; www.transporttreasury.co.uk*

Left. The handsome little waiting shelter on the Up platform at Evercreech Junction, photographed on 3 May 1964. We heard that the running-in boards at this legendary establishment were burned by the demolition people after the line had closed. It almost makes one cry – that 'Evercreech Junc' board would have looked absolutely superb on this writer's office wall. If one knew then what one knows now... *Photograph: P.Gomm; www.transporttreasury.co.uk*

Above. The tall Evercreech Junction South signal box was adjacent to the level crossing which took the railway over the A371 Shepton Mallet-Castle Cary road at the south end of the station. It had 26 levers. The level crossing itself is just out of view to the right. On the wall of the 'box is the customary warning: Passengers Must Cross The Line By The Foot Bridge. This picture was taken on 3 May 1964. *Photograph: P.Gomm; www.transporttreasury.co.uk*

Top left. LMS-built 2P 40634 stands on the centre road between the platforms at Evercreech Junction, awaiting its next piloting duty over the Mendip Hills. As train weights had increased – especially when Midland bogie corridor stock started to appear on through workings – the need for banking/piloting, especially on the heavy weekend and summer season trains, had become more intense. Between Evercreech Junction and Bath, the maximum load permitted for an unassisted engine was 200 tons (270 tons for the 'Black Fives', which first appeared on the S&D in 1938), but while such loading limits were often adequate for off-season weekday trains it could be a very different matter on summer Saturdays. On a typical summer Saturday there was usually a problem with the direction and the timing of the rush: the bulk of the northbound traffic (i.e. trains carrying holidaymakers returning from the South Coast) traversed the line in the morning, while the heaviest traffic heading southward to the coast traversed the line in the afternoon. Consequently, it was impossible to balance the majority of the assisting duties by having, say, a northbound pilot turn round at Bath and return as pilot to the next southbound train. The option of sending a pilot back to its starting point light engine was a non-starter, partly on the grounds of economy and partly due to additional track occupation. By the early 1950s (if not before) a solution of sorts had been found to the unevenness of banking and piloting requirements on summer Saturday peaks. As already explained, in the morning the majority of assistance was required by northbound trains, but Templecombe shed (ten miles to the south of Evercreech Junction) could not be expected to fill all the requirements and so additional engines had to be supplied by Bath. In order to reduce track occupation the Bath engines (usually 4-4-0s) were dispatched to Evercreech Junction piloting comparatively light-loaded trained such as the 8.15am and 9.55am locals from Green Park. In the northbound direction most pilot engines that were attached at Evercreech Junction worked through to Bath, but at the busiest times some of the assisting engines were detached at Binegar (having negotiated Masbury Summit) and then ran back tender-first to Evercreech Junction. *Photograph: Derek Clayton*

Middle left. 4F 44557, which had been built for the S&D Joint Committee in 1922, prepares to leave the Up platform at Evercreech Junction on 22 July 1958. The train is destined for Bath. Lurking almost out of view behind 44557 is a Highbridge branch train headed by Ivatt 2-6-2T 41296. As noted in one of our earlier photo captions, the Highbridge branch trains usually moved across to this siding so as to free up the platforms for through trains. The small station goods yard is behind the Down platform; in the siding far left is a Highbridge branch 'B' Set. The original turntable was also behind the Down platform, but it was resited in the fork of the Bath and Burnham lines circa 1910. *Photograph: R.C.Riley; www.transporttreasury.co.uk*

Bottom left. Ex-GWR '2215' class 0-6-0 3210 trundles into Evercreech Junction with the 2.20pm Highbridge-Templecombe on 7 September 1963. As a final word about Evercreech Junction (for now, at least), there was once a Royal visit – albeit a 'hush hush' one. All is explained by Mrs.Mary Stokes who posted the following recollection on the BBC 'Peoples War' archive: 'I lived in Ditcheat (a mile to the west of Evercreech Junction) on a farm. We frequently had army troops camped in the fields. On one very hot June day in 1940 when I was four years old, someone came to tell my father that King George VI was coming to see the troops. I presumed that this was to present medals to the men who had been involved in Dunkirk. I was taken along our track which led to a field alongside the road from Evercreech Junction station to see him as he travelled past in his car. I can remember that it was kept very secret and we were not allowed to tell anyone. Though one lady had heard that he was coming, and she telephoned her husband from the Railway Hotel to ask him to bring down her best hat.' *Photograph: David Idle; www.transporttreasury.co.uk*

PASSENGER TRAINS AT EVERCREECH JUNCTION
Peak summer Saturdays 1960
Departure times unless otherwise stated; 'Pass' denotes estimated time passing time of non-stop trains
Pass 3.45am Sheffield-Bournemouth
Pass 4.00am Derby-Bournemouth
Pass 4.30am Bradford-Bournemouth
Pass 5.15am Manchester-Bournemouth
7.24am Templecombe-Bath
Arr. 7.56am ex-Highbridge
8.14am Bristol-Bournemouth
8.15am Evercreech Jct-Highbridge
Arr. 8.46am ex-Templecombe
9.32am Bath-Templecombe
9.34am Bournemouth-Liverpool
9.43am Templecombe-Bath
9.55am Evercreech Jct-Highbridge
Pass 10.03am Bristol-Bournemouth
10.14am Bournemouth-Bradford
10.45am Highbridge-Templecombe
10.52am Bournemouth-Liverpool/Manchester
11.04am Bournemouth-Manchester *(Pines Express)*
11.05am Bristol-Bournemouth
11.20am Bournemouth-Leeds
Pass 11.30am Birmingham-Bournemouth
11.46am Bournemouth-Derby
12.03pm Bournemouth-Manchester
12.24pm Templecombe-Bath
12.42pm Bournemouth-Sheffield
1.02pm Birmingham-Bournemouth
1.10pm Exmouth/sidmouth-Cleethorpes
1.20pm Evercreech Jct-Highbridge *(unadvertised to Burnham-on-Sea)*
1.28pm Nottingham-Bournemouth
2.02pm Bournemouth-Nottingham
2.25pm Bath-Templecombe
3.05pm Bournemouth-Bristol
3.12pm Cleethorpes-Sidmouth/Exmouth
3.22pm Highbridge-Templecombe
3.35pm Sheffield-Bournemouth
3.55pm Bradford-Bournemouth
4.16pm Evercreech Jct-Templecombe
4.20pm Bournemouth-Bristol
Arr. 4.29pm ex-Templecombe
4.30pm Manchester-Bournemouth *(Pines Express)*
4.42pm Templecombe-Bath
4.56pm Liverpool-Bournemouth
5.00pm Evercreech Jct-Highbridge
5.00pm Highbridge-Templecombe
5.20pm Manchester-Bournemouth
5.53pm Bath-Templecombe
5.55pm Bournemouth-Bristol
6.02pm Evercreech Jct-Highbridge
Arr. 8.09pm ex-Highbridge *(from Burnham-on-Sea [unadvertised])*
8.26pm Bristol-Bournemouth
8.50pm Bournemouth-Bristol
9.15pm Templecombe-Bath
9.25pm Evercreech Jct-Highbridge
11.43pm Bath-Templecombe *(calls to set down if required)*

Wincanton

Left. The guard gives the 'right away' to the driver of the anonymous Standard Class 4 2-6-0 at the head of a northbound train at Wincanton in February 1964. The photographer recorded that four passengers (and some parcels) had got off the train and five passengers had joined. As mentioned earlier, the Somerset & Dorset was formed in 1862 by the amalgamation of the Somerset Central Railway and Dorset Central Railway; Wincanton had been the northernmost station on the section wholly owned by the Dorset Central. As for the town of Wincanton, it was described in Holiday Haunts as a '…tranquil little town situated at the bottom of Windmill Hill in the valley of the River Cale, surrounded by a green countryside of woods and hills extending into the Blackmore Vale country. With its pleasing Georgian and Victorian buildings it has a pleasantly old-world atmosphere, and is a veritable sun trap. In 1553 the inhabitants of the town were nearly decimated by the plague, but now (the early 1950s) the population is 2,380. The town is served by a spacious railway station which had calls by virtually every train except the 'Pines' and the other Summer Saturday long-distance through trains'. *Photograph: Peter Barnfield*

Bottom left. The exterior of Wincanton station, October 1956. A couple of splendid old wooden barrows are ready for action. After the railway closed the site of the station was smothered by a housing estate and, today, there are no remains of the railway whatsoever. One of the roads on the estate is called Pines Close, but that is the only hint of the site's former glory. *Photograph: Derek Clayton*

OFFICIAL RACE CARD   **ONE SHILLING**

Under N.H. Rules and the usual Rules and Regulations of the Wincanton Meetings

1/-

WINCANTON
Saturday, 24th August, 1963

STEWARDS :
GENERAL SIR RICHARD McCREERY, G.C.B., K.B.E., D.S.O., M.C.
THE EARL OF ILCHESTER
P. S. TORY, Esq., M.F.H.
H. W. DUFOSEE, Esq.

Stewards' Secretary : Lt.-Col. C. H. F. Coaker

Handicapper : Mr. W. H. Harley.   Starter : Major K. P. Wallis.
Judge : Mr. G. P. Roffe-Silvester.   Clerk of the Scales : Mr. J. R. H. Warren.
Hon. Medical Officers : Dr. E. M. Tustin, M.R.C.S.   Dr. D. Pickett.
Veterinary Surgeons : Major W. Blanshard, M.R.C.V.S.
Mr. G. L. Barker, M.R.C.V.S.

Clerk of the Course and Stakeholder :
Brigadier R. E. G. Carolin, Berry Horn House, Odiham, Nr. Basingstoke, Hants.

Next Meeting :
THURSDAY, 19th SEPTEMBER — First Race 2 p.m.'

DOGS ARE NOT PERMITTED ON THE COURSE, OR IN ANY OF THE ENCLOSURES

In **STEEPLE CHASES** leave all **RED** boards on **YOUR RIGHT**.
In **HURDLE RACES** leave all **WHITE** boards on **YOUR RIGHT**.

EDWIN SNELL & SONS LIMITED, YEOVIL

4972

WINCANTON
RENEWAL OF FOOTBRIDGE No.136

It was reported by Joint Conference minute No.697 that the condition of footbridge No.136 at Wincanton, which is of timber construction, was such as to require renewal of practically the whole structure, and that with a view to economy the Managements had concurred in a proposal to reconstruct the bridge in ferro-concrete, as shown on plan No.10/2264.D/W.15, at an estimated cost of £320.

Approved.

5062

WINCANTON:
IMPROVED GOODS OFFICE ACCOMMODATION

It was reported by minute No.884 of the Joint Conference that the Goods Office at Wincanton was totally inadequate for the accommodation of the necessary staff, from whom complaints had been received of the unpleasant conditions, particularly during hot weather, owing to the close proximity of stables and a refuse tip.

As the existing building could not be extended in a satisfactory manner it was recommended that improved accommodation be provided on another site, in accordance with the scheme shown on plan No.WD6/1729B submitted, at an estimated cost of £433, which included the installation of a lavatory basin with necessary drainage, gas lighting and radiators, furniture and linoleum floor covering.

The existing office would be utilised for the storage of old books and papers at present stacked on the goods shed platform.

Recommendation approved.

Top left. S&D Joint Committee minute, 4 November 1936

Bottom left. S&D Joint Committee minute, 2 November 1938

Templecombe

Class 4 2-6-0 76025 approaches Templecombe Lower with the 1.10pm Bournemouth West-Bristol on 7 September 1963. *Photograph: David Idle; www.transporttreasury.co.uk*

9F 92220 Evening Star – the very last steam locomotive to be built by British Railways – stands at the S&D platform at Templecombe Upper. It appears that a change of crew is underway. The picture came without a date, but as the engine was allocated to Bath for only a couple of months in the late summer of 1962 and again in the late summer of 1963 the date can be narrowed down somewhat. *Photograph: Paul Chancellor Collection*

As noted in other books in this series, trains were piloted out of Templecombe upper on to the main line at Templecombe No.2 Junction, from where they resumed their journey northwards or southwards. Here, Pannier Tank 3720 is ready to lead a southbound train out of the station; the train engine is at the other end. The reversal procedure at Templecombe was very tedious. One observer in the 1950s called the procedure a 'humiliating rigmarole', but the legendary E.L.Ahrons was even less charitable. In his legendary *Locomotive and Train Working in the Nineteenth Century* he recalled a journey from Wimborne to Bath in the late 1800s: '…having got to Templecombe the train proceeded to perform something in the nature of looping the loop. This was done by backing the train up the incline from the Somerset & Dorset line to the High Level South Western station, and I remember that they had backed halfway up when they found a goods train on the road, which they might have thought of before, with the result that the Somerset & Dorset express got tied up for half an hour before it could be extricated. I have called this train an express; really it was a so-called fast train of sorts which left Wimborne after breakfast-time and reached Bath too late for lunch and somewhat too early for tea'. *Photograph: Leslie Freeman; www.transporttreasury.co.uk*

A 'different to usual' view of Templecombe station, taken in October 1956. The picture was taken from Combe Throop Lane; we are looking westwards – the 'main line' part of the station is to the left (above the bridge under which the road passes) while the S&D's platform and connecting line is on the right. *Photograph: Derek Clayton*

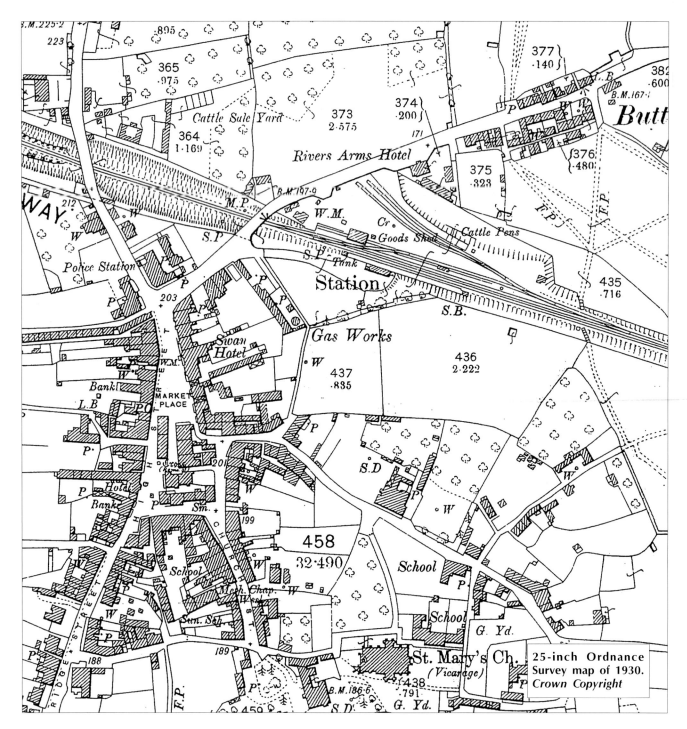

25-inch Ordnance Survey map of 1930. Crown Copyright

Top right. Sturminster Newton station, looking north, February 1966. The bridge at the far end of the station takes the Shaftesbury road (the B3091) over the railway. Many of the towns and villages served by the S&D had wonderfully rural-sounding names but, for many, Sturminster Newton took the prize. Indeed, one of its fans was John Betjeman, who celebrated it in his famous poem, Dorset: 'Rime Intrinsica, Fontmell Magna, Sturminster Newton and Melbury Bubb, whist upon whist upon whist upon whist drive, in Institute, Legion and Social Club. Horny hands that hold the aces which this morning held the plough – while Tranter Reuben, T.S.Eliot, H.G.Wells and Edith Sitwell lie in Mellstock Churchyard now...' ('Mellstock' is of course the fictional name that Thomas Hardy gave to his home parish of Stinsford in Dorset.) *J.G.Harrod & Co's Postal & Commercial Directory of Dorset & Wiltshire 1865* noted that Sturminster Newton was '...a market town, parish, and has a castle and also a railway station on the Dorset Central Railway, in the hundred and union of the same name, distant 108 miles from London. The church, St.Mary's, within about the last twenty years has been nearly rebuilt, and very considerably enlarged, at the sole expense of the late Rev.T.H.Lane Fox; it is in the Norman style, in the form of a cross. The living is a vicarage, in the gift of Lord Rivers, lord of the manor, and the tithes have been commuted for £712, with residence; the Rev. Richard Lowndes is the vicar. The Primitive Methodists have a chapel. The Wesleyans have a chapel and Sunday school. There are schools for children of both sexes and for infants, supported by voluntary subscriptions. On the Newton side of the river are the remains of an old castle, supposed to have been erected by the Romans; they consist of a keep, within a vallum and ditch, seated on a hill. The ground-plan was in the form of the letter D. There is a large camp, called Banbury. A Literary and Scientific Institution was established in 1850. There is a market every alternate Thursday, chiefly for cattle. The fairs are held on the 12th of May and 24th of October, at which is appointed the high constable of the hundred of Sturminster. The petty sessions of the division are held monthly here, The population in 1861 was 1,880, and the acreage 4,229. In the union of Sturminster there are twenty parishes. The workhouse is at Sturminster. Board meeting every Wednesday.' Today, Sturminster Newton – or 'Stur' as it is known to the locals – is still a smart and prosperous little market town. *Photograph: Peter Barnfield*

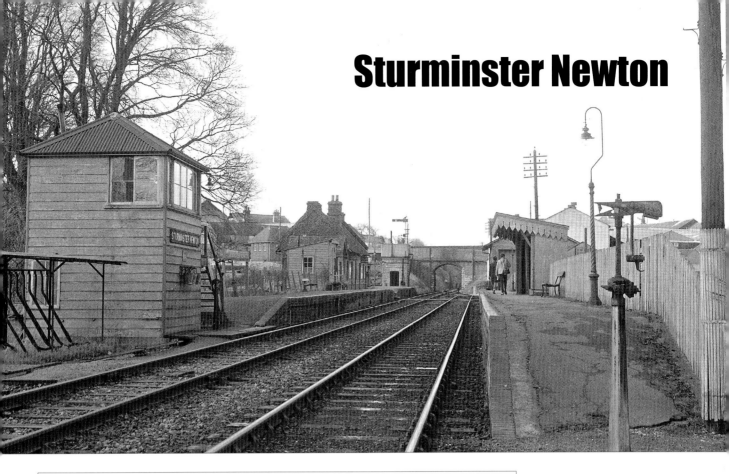

COPY.
S.R.16388.

MINISTRY OF TRANSPORT
4, Whitehall Gardens,
London, S.W.1.

24th June, 1932.

Sir,

      I have the honour to report for the information of the Minister of Transport that, in accordance with the Appointment of 18th December 1930, I made an inspection on 21st June 1932 of the new works at Sturminster Newton on the Somerset and Dorset Joint Railway.

      The connection at the west end of the station to the north siding, formerly trailing in the up line, has now been replaced by a connection facing in the down loop line. The new connection consists of 95 lb. material on Mendip ballast.

      At the same time a ground frame has been abolished and various alterations effected in the signals and their operation.

      The box contains an old frame of 12 levers to which 4 have been added, making 16 levers all in use, of which 2 are Push and Pull.

      The locking is correct and all necessary arms are repeated in the box.

      The works are complete and in good order and I recommend approval be given thereto.

                 I have the honour to be,
                      Sir,
                 Your obedient Servant,

                 (Sgd.) A.C. TRENCH.
                     Colonel.

The Secretary,
    Ministry of Transport.

RD.

Left. 47542 of Templecombe shunts in the yard at the rear of the Down platform at Sturminster Newton on 4 July 1961. A 'Jinty' was not a common sight at Sturminster Newton; indeed, a visitor to the town on 13 December 1958 had reported: '47542 was used three times during the week ending 13 December 1958 on the Templecombe-Blandford pick-up goods, but this unprecedented experiment does not seem to have been a success and has not been repeated since.' Given that unfavourable report, one assumes that, in this picture, the loco was deputising for the customary 3F 0-6-0 on the 11.05am Templecombe-Blandford pick-up goods. The herbaceous sidings on which the photographer is standing are those serving the Milk Marketing Board factory. The coming of the railway to the town in 1863 had been of great benefit to local dairy farmers as it meant that not only could fresh milk go to London, but calves could be sent anywhere in the country (for a flat fare of 2/6!) Consequently the many dairy farms in the Blackmore Vale became prosperous and much sought-after. *Photograph: R.C.Riley; www.transporttreasury.co.uk*

Bottom left. It is February 1966, and the fireman of Class 4 2-6-0 76005 collects the token at Sturminster Newton before resuming the journey to Bournemouth. The section between Templecombe and Blandford Forum had never been doubled, so at the beginning and end of each signalling section the tablet had to be exchanged. Most of the engines that were long-term residents on the S&D were fitted with Whitaker tablet exchanging apparatus (which has been described in other books in this series), but 76005, being a late-comer to the line, was not. In this picture, the end of the loop – the reversion to single track – can be seen in the distance. The presence of single-track sections not only required different signalling arrangements, but also presented bottlenecks where delays could occur. For much of the time this was largely hypothetical, but on summer Saturdays the traffic on the line was so intense that bottlenecks *did* cause problems. Since the closure of the railway much of the site of Sturminster Newton station has been incorporated in a car park and there are no railway relics to be seen. The old trackbed to the north of the station has been completely obliterated by housing developments but the trackbed to the south of the station site has been converted to a formal footpath-cum-cycleway – the North Dorset Trailway – which, with the recent opening of a new bridge near Fiddleford, now extends all the way through to Shillingstone. Do get your walking boots out – it's a smashing walk through beautiful countryside. *Photograph: Peter Barnfield*

STURMINSTER NEWTON.

Fouling single line:—

After an up train has drawn in clear to allow a down train to leave, it may be set back outside the home signal, provided the instructions contained in Regulation 16 of the Electric Train Tablet Regulations have been carried out.

In such cases the guard must ride back in the rear van, and the engine must not be detached from the train or any portion thereof, until it has been brought to a stand, and the guard has applied the van brake (and also any wagon brakes and sprags if necessary), to prevent the detached portion of the train from again moving.

Milk Factory Siding:—

Bogie vehicles must not be shunted into the Milk Factory siding, and engines must, whenever practicable, be coupled up to the vehicles with the engine clear of the crossing.

Right. 7F 53807 stands at Bailey Gate on 25 August 1964. The rear brake van has been detached, so one assumes that the solitary van is about to be taken off or, alternatively, that some other wagons had already been taken off. The incoming vehicles were probably for the United Dairies (originally Carters & Dorset Modern Dairies) factory on the north side of the station. The milk traffic from the factory was a steady source of revenue for the railway; incidentally, Bailey Gate was one of two stations on the S&D main line which dealt with bulk milk traffic – the other was Wincanton. *Photograph: Paul Chancellor Collection*

Bottom right. An empty Bailey Gate station, 4 July 1961. Milk vans stand in the dock behind the Down platform. Note the station nameboards on each platform – the one on the Down platform announces that the station if 'for Sturminster Marshall' but the one on the Up platform does not. *Photograph: R.C.Riley; www.transporttreasury.co.uk*

Below. A lovely study of a northbound train – we believe it is the 7.10am Bournemouth-Templecombe – pulling into Bailey Gate in February 1966, only a couple of weeks or so before the withdrawal of passenger services on the S&D. The engine is in an abysmal condition; it has lost its smokebox numberplate, the number now being written with chalk. It is not easy to read, but our money is on 80011 which had been transferred to Bournemouth in October 1965 and, although transferred to Guildford in January 1966, returned to Bournemouth a few weeks later. *Photograph: Peter Barnfield*

Bailey Gate a

Corfe Mullen

We are looking eastwards at Corfe Mullen on 5 July 1964. Corfe Mullen Junction is a short distance beyond the level crossing; the junction signal box is on the Up side of the level crossing which takes an unclassified road to The Knoll over the railway. The photographer was standing on a bridge which took the unclassified road to Henbury Plantation. *Photograph: Leslie Freeman; www.transporttreasury.co.uk*

After taking the previous picture, the photographer walked about ¼-mile eastwards to the bridge which took the B3074 Corfe Mullen-Broadstone road over the railway. He is still looking eastwards; Corfe Mullen Junction itself is just behind us. The line on the left is the old line to Wimborne; the one on the right is the cut-off line to Broadstone which opened in 1885. Prior to the opening of the cut-off line S&D trains used to run to Wimborne where they had to change direction before proceeding to Bournemouth, but despite the availability of the cut-off line from 1885 some S&D passenger trains continued to use the old line to Wimborne until 1920. Goods services were not withdrawn from that line until 1933 and, even then, the 1½-mile section between Corfe Mullen and Carters Siding was retained for the clay traffic from the latter point until September 1959. That stretch of line was subsequently used for wagon storage for a few more years. This view might have been rather different: in 1925 plans were made for doubling the Corfe Mullen-Broadstone line but, as the history books (and this picture) show, that did not happen. *Photograph: Leslie Freeman; www.transporttreasury.co.uk*

Bournemouth West

7F 2-8--0 53807 and 4F 0-6-0 44558 stand at Bournemouth West on Sunday 7 June 1964. The presence of so many enthusiasts on the platform is a give-away: the locos were not on an ordinary working, but on the Home Counties Railway Society special. The rail tour had started at Waterloo and had run to Bournemouth, where the S&D locos had taken over. The organisers had hoped that the second loco would be 53809, but that engine had been condemned the previous month so the 4F had been called upon as a replacement. Nevertheless, it was significant that 53807 and 44558 had actually been built for the S&D, and this special working was the last occasion on which a pair of ex-S&D locos worked together on their 'home' line. *Photograph: D.T.Flook*

As pointed out in other books in this series, Bournemouth West was not only the end of the line for S&D trains as, prior to the changes at Bournemouth in the early autumn of 1965, virtually all of the Southern trains which started or terminated in the town did so at West station. Consequently, there was empty stock to be moved in to and out of the platforms, and for many years the smashing little M7 0-4-4Ts were regularly used on these duties. Here, 30127 pulls away with a rake of empties in the low evening sunshine of 20 August 1962. It is carrying part of a vestibule shield above the buffer beam. *Photograph: B.J.Wadey*

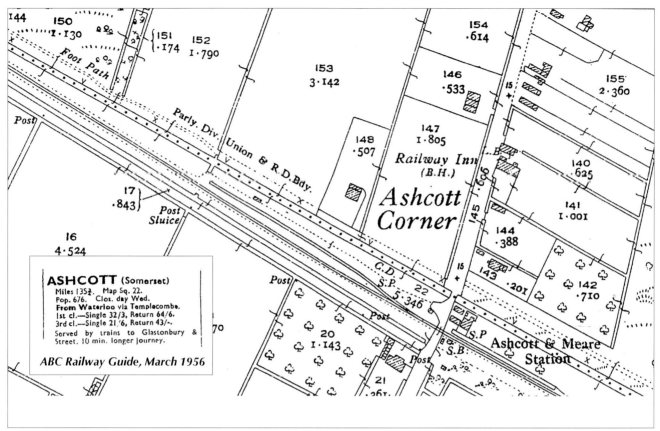

25-inch Ordnance Survey map of 1903. *Crown Copyright*

'The branch' – Evercreech Junction to Burnham-on-Sea
Ashcott

5062

Prior to 1876 Ashcott station had been named Ashcott & Meare. That dual title was not a case of over-aggrandisement, as the station was between those two villages. That said, neither of those villages was exactly close to the railway – Ashcott was 1¾ miles to the south and Meare was 1¼ miles to the north. The reason for abbreviating the title to Ashcott is unclear, but had Brunel built the railway the station would very probably have been named Ashcott Road. Indeed, the road which crossed the line at the west end of the station was the minor lane between Ashcott and Meare. This picture was taken on 2 March 1956. The goods siding on the west side of the level crossing can be seen. *Photograph: R.M.Casserley*

36

Below. This closer view of the level crossing and the neat little ground frame cabin at Ashcott was taken circa 1950. This cabin, which had ten levers, was installed in June 1902 to replace the previous cabin of 1879. The level crossing gates were manually operated. Ashcott was one of three stations on this stretch of railway which dealt with peat traffic – the others were Shapwick and Edington. There were also private sidings for peat traffic: Petfu Sidings, ¾-mile east of Ashcott, and Alexander's Siding, for the Eclipse Peat Company (later Fisons), ½-mile west of Ashcott. Until the mid-1950s up to ten wagons of peat were dispatched each day from Ashcott station and a similar number of vans from Alexander's Siding. However, when BR refused the Eclipse Peat Company's application for a fixed rate for sending all their traffic by rail, the peat company started to make a gradual switch to road transport. The Eclipse company had its own 2ft gauge railway, and this crossed the S&D line on the level about ½-mile west of Ashcott station. The crossing was not protected by signals, and the perils of this were demonstrated on 19 August 1949. 3F 0-6-0 No.3260 (which had not yet received its designated BR number, 43260) was hauling the 8.00am mixed train from Glastonbury to Bridgwater and, near Ashcott, it collided with one of the Eclipse Peat Company's small petrol-engined Motor Rail locomotives which had stalled on the crossing. The driver of the peat company's locomotive had run along the S&D line to give warning, but it was a foggy morning and the driver of the 3F did not see him until it was too late. The 3F left the rails and finished up in the rhine where it lay for several weeks accumulating a considerable deposit of pond weed in the cab. Lifting and repairing was considered uneconomic, so the engine was cut up on the spot into 4-ton pieces which were duly dispatched for scrap. The accident brought home the fact that operations at the crossing had been rather haphazard, so to infuse some discipline into the crossing procedure the Southern Region subsequently insisted on telephone communication with the signal cabin. *Photograph: Joe Moss Collection; courtesy Roger Carpenter*

COPY.
(S.B.16388.

MINISTRY OF TRANSPORT
4, Whitehall Gardens,
London, S.W.1.

24th June, 1932.

Sir,

I have the honour to report for the information of the Minister of Transport that, in accordance with the Appointment of 18th December 1930, I made an inspection on 21st June 1932 of the new works at Sturminster Newton on the Somerset and Dorset Joint Railway.

The connection at the west end of the station to the north siding, formerly trailing in the up line, has now been replaced by a connection facing in the down loop line. The new connection consists of 95 lb. material on Mendip ballast.

At the same time a ground frame has been abolished and various alterations effected in the signals and their operation.

The box contains an old frame of 12 levers to which 4 have been added, making 16 levers all in use, of which 2 are Push and Pull.

The locking is correct and all necessary arms are repeated in the box.

The works are complete and in good order and I recommend approval be given thereto.

I have the honour to be,
Sir,
Your obedient Servant,

(Sgd.) A.C. TRENCH.
Colonel.

The Secretary,
Ministry of Transport.

RD.

S&D Joint Committee minute, 6 February 1935

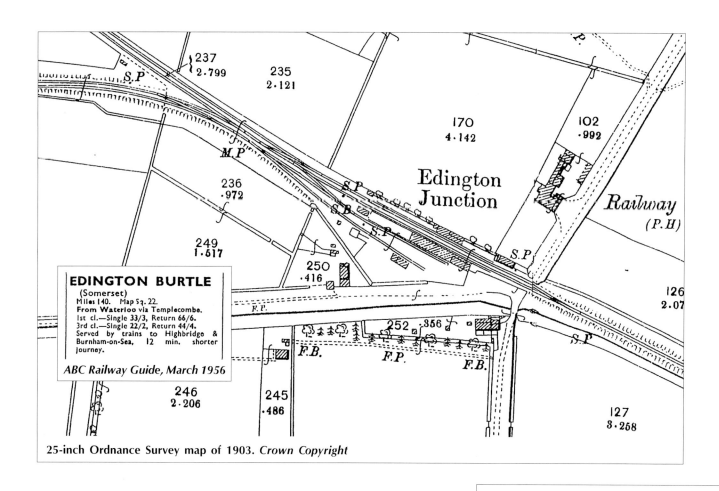

EDINGTON BURTLE

(Somerset)
Miles 140. Map Sq. 22.
From Waterloo via Templecombe.
1st cl.—Single 33/3, Return 66/6.
3rd cl.—Single 22/2, Return 44/4.
Served by trains to Highbridge &
Burnham-on-Sea, 12 min. shorter
journey.

ABC Railway Guide, March 1956

237
2·799

235
2·121

170
4·142

102
·992

S.P

M.P

236
·972

Edington
Junction

Railway
(P.H)

249
1·517

250
·416

252   ·356

F.P.

126
2·07

F.P.

F.B.

F.B.

246
2·206

245
·486

127
3·258

25-inch Ordnance Survey map of 1903. *Crown Copyright*

Right. The railway station for the village of Edington was not actually in the village of that name, but in the hamlet of Edington Burtle, about two miles to the north. This explains why it was originally named – in a perversely Brunel-esque fashion – Edington Road. The station was also intended to serve the villages of Catcott and Chilton Polden which, like Edington, nestled on the northern side of the Polden Hills facing the pancake-flat Somerset Levels. However, as the combined populations of Edington, Catcott and Chilton Polden in the late 1800s was only about 1,500, the scope for passenger traffic was still rather meagre. Furthermore, the three villages were much closer to the Glastonbury-Bridgwater road (later the A39) than they were to the railway, so when motor buses eventually started to ply along the main road the railway faced competition for the little traffic that was on offer. When the station became the junction for the newly-opened Bridgwater branch in 1890 it was renamed Edington Junction. The Bridgwater branch lost its passenger services in December 1952 and in June the following year the station was renamed Edington Burtle. The Bridgwater branch remained open for goods traffic for a couple more years, but closed completely in 1954. This meant that Edington Burtle station now had less work to handle (or should we say *even* less work?) so the layout was much simplified: in February 1956 the crossing loop, Down (eastbound) platform and all but one of the sidings were taken out of use and the signalling dispensed with. This picture shows the 'post-simplification' scene at the station in October 1956; somewhat unnecessarily, the disproportionately large platform canopy had been left in situ. We are looking east towards Evercreech. The level crossing at the far end of the station took the minor lane between the villages of Edington (to the right) and Edington Burtle (to the left) over the railway. The crossing gates were worked by hand but were locked by the ground frame which had replaced the old signal box. The house on the left by the crossing is for the station staff. *Photograph: Derek Clayton*

Top right. If Edington Burtle station looked rather forlorn when the previous picture was taken in 1956, by the time this picture was taken in the summer of 1965 the place was in an even sorrier state. We are looking westwards towards Highbridge. The platform buildings and the other woodwork seem to have been a paintbrush-free zone for years, and even the station house in the right foreground looks desperately uncared-for. But the whole of the platform canopy is still there, ready to provide shelter for more passengers than the station would have had to deal with in a month or more. *Photograph: Peter Barnfield*

Edington Burtle

40

Left. After the removal of the abandoned tracks and equipment from Edington Burtle in the mid-1950s Mother Nature made an enthusiastic take-over bid, so that by the time this picture was taken on 12 July 1961 the station looked very herbaceous. We are looking west towards Highbridge. 3F 0-6-0 43682 waits to depart. The chances of its train having picked up any passengers are pretty remote. Indeed, a visitor to the station in the early 1960s commented that 'passengers have dwindled to a mere handful and parcels are just one or two each day. An occasional wagon of coal comes in for Symes, but little else. Water churns for the crossing keepers along the line are still brought in by train, either on the engines themselves or in the brake compartments of passenger trains'. *Photograph: Peter Barnfield*

Bottom left. One aspect of the 'rationalisation' at Edington in February 1956 was the removal of the old 39-lever signal box. It was replaced by this 3-lever ground frame which controlled the connection to the remaining siding and the locking for the level crossing gates at the east end of the station. So the 'newness' of the frame is not deceptive – when this picture was taken in October 1956 the frame had been in situ for only eight months. An item of interest in the background on the left is the romantically-named South Drain, one of the many man-made waterways which help to drain the Somerset Levels. (The term 'Levels' is not an exaggeration, as the land is very, very flat indeed; the highest point on the Levels is Burtle Hill, a not very staggering 23 feet above sea level.) To the best of our limited knowledge, at this point the South Drain is more or less on the alignment of the old Glastonbury Canal. The canal opened in 1833 but it had a very short working life as almost all of it was abandoned in 1854, two years before the railway line between Highbridge and Glastonbury opened. *Photograph: Derek Clayton*

Below. This fine array of posters was to be found alongside the entrance to Edington Burtle station in October 1956. Given the station's dearth of passengers, one wonders if BR's advertising bods were familiar with the term 'target audience'. But if nothing else, the posters gave a heaven-sent excuse for retaining the splendid old notice board, complete with its 'Somerset & Dorset Joint Railway' heading. As for the village of Edington, in Maxwell Fraser's 1934 guide book entitled *Somerset* (which was written as a publicity organ for the GWR, not the S&D!) it is explained: 'Edington boldly claims to be the site of the battle of Ethandune (the other village of Edington – the one near Bratton in Wiltshire – makes the same claim), but the fact that Guthrum's forces were concentrated in the Poldens, and that Alfred's army was gathered in the Quantocks under Earl Odda, and that the battle was followed by the Treaty of Wedmore, and Guthrum's baptism at Aller, combine to make the claim of this Somerset village perfectly plausible, and Wiltshire's claim entirely unassailable'. Somerset 1, Wiltshire 0. *Photograph: Derek Clayton*

Left. Johnson 0-4-4T 58072 alongside the Highbridge water tank, 9 August 1953. The S&D's own 0-4-4Ts were withdrawn in the 1930s and '40s but several of the LMS's Johnson 0-4-4Ts were drafted in as replacements. In the mid-1940s there were five at Highbridge and two at Templecombe (and a further three at Bath which were available for the S&D line if required), but by January 1948 the stud comprised four at Highbridge (plus one at Bath). The ones at Highbridge were used mainly on the Wells and Bridgwater branches and also the Highbridge-Burnham locals, but the withdrawal of passenger services from those lines in 1951 and 1952 deprived the characterful engines of their principal duties. Nevertheless, three – 58051, 58072 and 58086 – were retained at Highbridge and were occasionally used on the branch to Evercreech Junction.   A visitor to the branch in 1953 reported that, on 28 February, 58086 was on the 1.15pm Evercreech Jct-Highbridge; it was '...running about 20 minutes late, and in consequence the 2.15pm Highbridge-Templecombe was delayed for 15 minutes before leaving Highbridge. The latter was formed of 58072 (condenser fitted) and two LMS non-corridors, both conveying 20-25 passengers'. In May 1953 Highbridge's stud of 0-4-4Ts was boosted from three to four by the arrival of 58073. However, by the

```
4840                    HIGHBRIDGE WORKSHOPS
                     LETTING OF VACANT PREMISES

            The Joint Conference by its minute No.440 reported that the
     disused Carriage & Wagon Erecting Shop at Highbridge had been leased to Mr.
     Ashford for a period of three years at a rental of £50 per annum, plus rates,
     for use as a piggery.    During the past three months additional traffic
     to the extent of £250 has been put on rail by Mr. Ashford, and it is
     anticipated that it will amount to £1,000 per annum.

            In order to render the premises suitable for occupation and use
     by Mr. Ashford, with the approval of the Managements necessary repairs to
     the roof of the building have been carried out at an estimated cost of £66,
     and check rails, necessitated by the use for vehicular traffic of the level
     crossing by which the only road access to the premises is obtained, provided
     at an estimated cost of £51.

            Mr. Ashford complains that by reason of the insufficient strength
     and width of bridge No.280A which spans a water course and is situate on
     the only road access he is unable to reach the premises by motor lorry.
     Improvement of the bridge will in any case be essential before the other
     disused workshops can be leased and it is recommended that it be put into
     a satisfactory condition forthwith, the estimated cost being £130.

                                    Action of the Managements confirmed
                                    and recommendation approved.
```

S&D Joint Committee minute, 2 May 1934

mid-1950s they had lost most of their duties on the Highbridge branch to 3F 0-6-0s, so it came as little surprise when 58072 and 58073 were placed in store in 1955. Those two – and 58051 – were withdrawn the following year. Those three engines claimed a couple of 'lasts': 58051 had been the last Derby-built member of the class (the remaining engines had all been built by Dübs & Co of Glasgow) while 58072 had been the last condenser-fitted example to have survived, its condensers having been left on despite its transfer away from the London area many years earlier. Following those withdrawals, the only 0-4-4T left on the S&D was 58086. As we saw in one of the other books in this series, in May 1959 58086 was sent to Bath for storage. Following the withdrawal of 58065 from Lincoln in October of that year, 58086 was left as the very last Johnson 0-4-4T in existence. Sadly, it seems that this last survivor never returned to action. It was withdrawn in August 1960 and passed through Derby for the last time on 6 September, being hauled 'dead' by 45323. It finished up at Gorton where it was cut up in early October. *Photograph: Ivo Peters*

Bottom. 3Fs 43218 and 43419 stand outside the engine shed at Highbridge on 9 August 1953. Ten 3Fs had been built for the S&D – five in 1896 and five more in 1902 – but some of those native engines were later transferred away while others came in from elsewhere. 43218 was one of the natives – it had been built for the S&D in 1902 and survived until April 1960. 43419 was one of the incomers; it had been built for the Midland Railway in 1892, had later routinely passed to the LMS, and did not come to the S&D until November 1949 when it was transferred from Bristol to Highbridge. In the mid-1950s the 3Fs had some of their regular duties taken over by 4Fs and Ivatt 2-6-2Ts which had themselves been ousted from main line duties by Standard 2-6-0s and 4-6-0s. The 3Fs were subsequently used mainly on the Highbridge branch. Nevertheless, they proved to be remarkably tenacious and a couple (43216 and 43682) remained on the S&D – allocated to Templecombe – until they were condemned in early September 1962, by which time there were only a handful of the once numerous class left anywhere in Britain. 43419 had, however, departed for the great scrap yard in the sky a few years earlier, having been withdrawn from Templecombe in September 1958. *Photograph: Ivo Peters*

```
4874                    HIGHBRIDGE WORKSHOPS

            Referring to minute No.4861 of this Committee, it was reported by
     minute No.514 of the Joint Conference that the Burnham-on-Sea Urban District
     Council were not in favour of dealing with any of the land required on an
     option basis, but were willing, subject to the confirmation of the appropriate
     Government Department, to sell to the Joint Committee the strip of land
     coloured red on the plan submitted, containing an area of 599 square yards,
     for the sum of £10, which would enable the existing approach road to the
     Committee's premises to be widened to 20 feet as and when required.

                                    The acquisition of the strip of
     S&D Joint Committee minute, 6 February 1935    land in question approved.
```

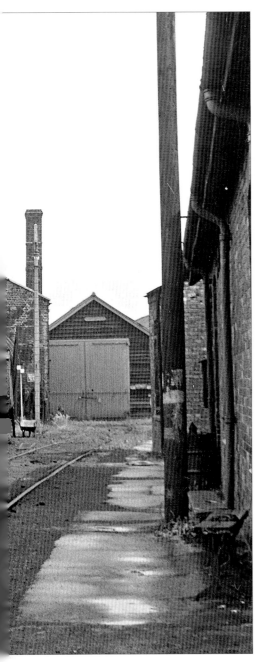

Left. Although Highbridge was officially closed in May 1959, this was the scene on 12 July 1961 – 3F 0-6-0 43682 and a 4F were on shed. A decade earlier it had been unusual to see a 4F at Highbridge, but in the mid-1950s they were displaced from the S&D main line by Standard 2-6-0s and 4-6-0s and their new-found alternative duties included the branch. The presence of the open wagon on the right-hand shed road confirms that, by this time, coaling was done direct from a wagon. The roof of the shed building confirms that it had four roads – two under each gable. However, the two left-hand roads had been taken out of use by 1922 and that portion of the shed had subsequently been separated from the rest of the building by a wooden partition. In later years it was used to store bulky items such as drums of oil, brake blocks, firebars, springs and the like. *Photograph: Peter Barnfield*

Bottom left. Highbridge shed was officially closed on 11 May 1959 and its remaining duties on the Evercreech Junction-Highbridge branch were taken over by Templecombe. However, Highbridge continued to stable a couple of engines overnight – usually one for freight and one for passenger work – until the closure of the S&D in March 1966. This picture, which was taken on a summer Sunday in 1959, shows the shelter which had been built over the coal wagon road. A wagon is positioned under the shelter, as if to confirm that the depot was not totally defunct. The two vintage coaches are probably in departmental use. Writing in *Sempahore*, the journal of the Avon Valley Railway, Michael Wyatt describes a visit to Highbridge shed in its later years: 'The shed, formerly 71J, was situated some way from the station on the south side of the line to Evercreech Junction. Walking from the end of the Down platform you would pass the site of the old carriage and wagon works, razed to the ground in the mid-fifties, just the track set in concrete now left as a bleak reminder. The number of engines on shed always seemed to be far in excess of the number required to work the traffic on the branch. 43216 together with 43356 would perhaps be gently simmering outside the shed office, and 41241 and 41243 would be inside the shed building, out of steam awaiting the next turn of duty. The locomotive works were still standing at this time – twenty-eight years after the last engine had left. It did not need too much imagination to bring it back to life and just for a moment to visualise a fine array of Prussian Blue S&D locomotives fresh from overhaul, ready again to attack the Mendip slopes. Dotted around the various buildings were reminders of the works former glory in the form of neat cast notices reading: "SDJR These buckets must be full of water and used only in case of fire. Any infringement of this order will be severely dealt with. By Order". Highbridge works was, to quote John Betjeman, "a faded Swindon, a forgotten Crewe". Just outside the old machine shops was the turntable which was still in use. This also had a cast iron notice which solemnly proclaimed "This turntable must be pulled and NOT pushed". After turning engines would go on shed for attention which included watering, oiling, ash clearing and coaling. Coaling at Highbridge was a rather primitive affair in as much as the coal had to be shovelled from a nearby wagon into a skip and then hoisted to the bunker, the coal then being released into the bunker of the engine. On the LMS 2-6-2 Ivatt tanks this was a particularly hazardous job as the bunker tops were narrow and so a good portion of the coal ended up on the track bed. In the meantime 43216 had moved off shed down to the station; the signal appeared to come off automatically from what looked like an unmanned signal box...' *Photograph: Peter Barnfield*

5282

5th February, 1947

HIGHBRIDGE MOTIVE POWER DEPOT
PROPOSED DISMANTLING OF SHED

It was reported by Joint Conference minute 1172 that, the timber extension of the main locomotive shed at Highbridge was in a bad state of repair and should be dismantled.   The Mutual Improvements class room at present partitioned off at the extreme end of the extension would require to be transferred to the main shed building.   It was also necessary to effect repairs to the roof of the main building, and authority was requested for carrying out the complete scheme at an estimated cost of £410 after allowing £46 for the value of recovered materials.

An immediate saving in repair and repainting work of approximately £250 would be effected, and a future saving in maintenance and renewal charges of £40 per annum.

Approved.

S&D Joint Committee minute, 5 February 1947

A splendid line-up of Johnson 0-4-4Ts – 58088, 58086 and a.n.other – at Highbridge on 17 August 1952. The contraption on the right of the picture is the coaling crane, small tubs of coal being hoisted by means of a crane so that their contents could be tipped into locomotive tenders or bunkers below. As a full tub was hoisted, an empty one was lowered. In the mid-1950s a corrugated iron shelter was erected on the coal wagon road to prevent coal dust from blowing everywhere. That problem had become more acute since the 1950s when soft Welsh coal had been used instead of Somerset coal. *Photograph: Ivo Peters*

The S&D's own locomotive works at Highbridge had closed in 1930. Part of the old erecting shop was retained for a few years as an auxiliary repair shop for the running shed; one of its regular jobs was to deal with hot boxes – Bath shed was unable to deal with these. However, the old shear legs were condemned in 1947 and, from then on, the only repairs dealt with were those which could be done at the running shed itself. Nevertheless, most of the works buildings remained standing until the 1960s. This picture was taken in the summer of 1959. In the foreground is the turntable; the herbaceous condition of its surroundings was not a direct legacy of the running shed having closed – it had been like this for several years. *Photograph: Peter Barnfield*

The final years

Following the nationalisation of the railways in 1948 the entire S&D line was operated by the Southern Region, and although the Western Region took over responsibility for administrative and commercial matters on the Bath-Cole section in 1950, the Southern retained responsibility for operations. Outwardly, things seemed little different. However, in February 1958 the WR took over the operations on the Bath-Henstridge section of the line, and this turned out to be a blow from which the S&D was never to recover.

Those who used and worked on the line feared the worst from the WR take-over, as the WR (like its predecessor, the GWR) had no real understanding of how vital the S&D was to the communities it served. Indeed, very soon after taking over, the WR management made no secret of the fact that it would line to close the Bath-Templecombe section, together with the connection from Mangotsfield to Bath. However, the WR's wishes did not curry favour with its neighbours, the Southern and the London Midland Regions: the SR did not want to be left with a dead-end branch from Bournemouth to Templecombe, and the LMR was alarmed about the possibility of having to drive new paths through an already congested timetable for its through summer traffic to and from Bournemouth. So the WR bided its time.

Given the circumstances the WR kept fairly quiet about its desire to close much of the S&D and, whenever questions were asked, the official party line was that it 'did not intend to close the S&D in the near future' but, ominously, it declined to state what it regarded as the 'near future'. Local people who depended on the railway were placed in a difficult position: as closure had not been announced, there was no mechanism for official objections. Nevertheless, the local support for the line was considerable and conspicuous. The WR feared that, as the support for the line increased, the more difficult it would be to effect closure, so it embarked on a process of 'running down'. This involved reducing the level of services and, in certain cases, altering the times of trains so that they were less useful to the public, sometimes by failing to make convenient connections with other trains. The idea was that a 'less useful' level of services would result in reduced usage of the line, so that when closure was eventually applied for, figures could be produced to prove that the line did not pay. Unfortunately, the tactic was not new; it had worked elsewhere.

The run-down started with a vengeance in 1962. At the end of the summer timetable the long-distance through trains to and from Bournemouth were diverted away from the line – the longest-distance trains that remained were between Bristol and Bournemouth. The diverted trains included the 'Pines Express'; as from the start of the winter timetable on 10 September 1962 the train was routed via Southampton and Oxford. The last 'Pines' on the S&D the previous Saturday, the 8th,

Bulleid Pacifics 34006 *Bude* **and 34057** *Biggin Hill* **stand at Bath shed on 5 March 1966. These two locos had taken over the LCGB's rail tour from Evercreech Junction and had brought it into Bath. They took the train out of Green Park at 4.07pm and brought it into Bournemouth Central at 6.51pm. There they were relieved by a Merchant Navy for the run back to Waterloo.**
Photograph: David Idle; www.transporttreasury.co.uk

<u>TRANSPORT ACT 1962 : SECTION 56(9)</u>

REPORT OF THE TRANSPORT USERS CONSULTATIVE COMMITTEE FOR
THE SOUTH EASTERN AREA ON THE PROPOSAL OF BRITISH
RAILWAYS (WESTERN AND SOUTHERN REGIONS) TO WITHDRAW THE
<u>PASSENGER TRAIN SERVICE ON THE SOMERSET AND DORSET LINE</u>

Minister of Transport,
St. Christopher House,
Southwark Street,
London, S.E.1.   2 4 DEC 1963

Sir,

    I have the honour to present my Committee's report on the proposal to close
that part of this railway as lies within the County of Dorset.

<u>THE PROPOSAL</u>

1. British Railways' Proposal in this case (the Heads of Information for which
are attached at Appendix 1) in so far as this Committee are concerned is to
withdraw the passenger train service between Bristol (Temple Meads), Bath (Green
Park) and Bournemouth West, most of which line (i.e. between Bath and Broadstone)
constituted the former Somerset and Dorset Joint Line and is hereinafter referred
to as "the S. & D."

2. That part of the line running north-westward from Henstridge (see Plan in
Appendix 1) is mainly in Somerset, with a small part in Gloucestershire, and is
within the South Western Area, whose Committee are making a separate report to you.'

<u>DESCRIPTION OF THE LINE IN DORSET</u>

3. The S. & D. enters Dorset between Henstridge and Stalbridge stations and
proceeds to Broadstone, there joining the line from Brockenhurst via Ringwood and
from Salisbury via Fordingbridge, over which the trains continue on to Poole and
Bournemouth. Passenger services on the Ringwood and Fordingbridge lines are also
proposed for withdrawal and have been the subject of a report to you by this
Committee on 5th November, 1963.

4. The S. & D. (in Dorset) serves the towns of Sturminster Newton (pop. 1,958)
and Blandford Forum (pop. 3,490) and possesses five stations, all well situated in
relation to the communities they serve. These five stations, together with the
approximate number of persons using them daily according to the April census,
are as follows (Note. - Stalbridge to Bournemouth is down):-

	Down Trains		Up Trains	
	Joining	Alighting	Joining	Alighting
Stalbridge	14	9	6	22
Sturminster Newton	58	30	34	60
Shillingstone	35	16	16	22
Blandford Forum	67	78	103	70
Bailey Gate (for Sturminster Marshall)	13	1	3	12

    As mentioned in para. 3, at Broadstone the S. & D. joins the line from
Brockenhurst and Salisbury, and the number of passengers daily using the S. & D.
trains at the stations thence to Bournemouth is as follows:-

	Down Trains		Up Trains	
	Joining	Alighting	Joining	Alighting
Broadstone	13	7	11	11
Creekmoor Halt	43	1	1	39
Poole	5	97	74	22
Parkstone	1	1	3	3
Branksome	3	2	4	2
Bournemouth West	-	76	74	-

5. At Templecombe, two stations north of Stalbridge, the S. & D. crosses the main
line between Waterloo and the West of England, and there connection is made with
trains to and from London and Exeter and beyond.

6. Templecombe station, however, is itself proposed for closure in the Beeching
Plan, and British Railways have recently announced in the Press plans for a further
reshaping of their system involving the closure of some trunk routes. There are
two trunk routes between London and the West Country - one from Paddington via
Reading and Westbury and the other from Waterloo via Salisbury and Templecombe -
and at our hearing it was suggested that one or the other of these two routes might
in due course be proposed for closure.

7. In the event of the closure of the S. & D. certain alternative bus services are proposed for passengers from eastern Dorset to London and to the West and are referred to in para. 24(i) of this Report. They will run to and from Gillingham (the next station east of Templecombe) in order to connect there with trains on the main line between Waterloo and Exeter, and their potential usefulness and the Committee's conclusions thereon are based on the assumption that this main line will continue to exist.

8. In addition to the connection at Templecombe referred to in para. 5, the S. & D. forms a through route from Bournemouth, Poole and eastern Dorset to Bath, Bristol, South Wales, the Midlands and the North.

TRAIN SERVICE

(a) Local Services in Dorset

9. 7 trains run daily in each direction on weekdays between Templecombe and Bournemouth, together with a late evening train at 10.0 p.m. on Saturdays from Bournemouth to Templecombe. The trains generally call at all stations. There is no Sunday service.

(b) Through services

10. Of the trains mentioned in the preceeding paragraph, 4 down and 3 up trains run through between Bristol and Bournemouth. One of them - the 11.40 a.m. Bournemouth to Bristol - is semi-fast, journey time 3 hours, but the corresponding down train - the 3.35 p.m. Bristol to Bournemouth - stops at more stations and takes 3½ hours, whilst the remaining trains in reach direction generally take 3¾/4 hours between Bristol and Bournemouth.

11. The 11.40 a.m. Bournemouth to Bristol makes a reasonable connection at Mangotsfield with the 2.40 p.m. express from Bristol to Gloucester, Birmingham and beyond. Otherwise connections to and from these towns are generally made via Bristol, with consequent longer journey time from and to the S. & D.

12. For many years a daily fast service in each direction over the S. & D. was provided by the "Pines Express", which ran between Bournemouth and Manchester and Liverpool via Birmingham. From 10th September, 1962, however, this train was routed via Basingstoke and Oxford; journey times between Bournemouth and Birmingham and beyond by this route today are generally shorter than when the train ran over the S. & D., so there is no hardship to passengers to and from Bournemouth; journey times to and from Poole are however rather longer than before but not seriously so. The S. & D. however is still the direct rail route from Bournemouth to the Bath, Bristol and Gloucester area, and from Blandford and north Dorset it is the direct route to these towns and also to Birmingham and beyond.

(c) Train loadings

13. The loadings of the trains given in the Heads of Information indicate that the first two morning trains into Poole and Bournemouth carry loads of some 50/80 passengers on the Dorset section of their journey; others go in during the day, often with prams, returning mainly on the 3.40 p.m. and 5.30 p.m. trains from Bournemouth West, which each carry some 40/60 people; on summer Saturdays loadings may exceed 100. Other trains are much more lightly loaded.

14. The Committee are unable to say what proportion of these passengers are making through journeys from and to Bath and beyond or via Templecombe, but the Line Manager of British Railways (Southern Region) suggested that the majority would probably be making local journeys.

FINANCIAL EFFECT OF CLOSURE

15. The financial information relating to the closure is given in Appendix G of the Heads of Information. This refers to the proposal as a whole - not just the Dorset section - and shows an excess of direct costs over revenue of £290,000 per annum. It was however pointed out that there are no diesel trains on any part of the lines proposed for closure, and the movement costs are therefore high because they relate entirely to steam operation.

16. Moreover, it was contended by many objectors that the line had been deliberately run down in recent years. The gradual contraction of services, the diversion of the "Pines Express" (see para. 12), the lack of publicity of the train service or of apparent efforts to attract traffic and the diversion of freight traffic from the line were cited as evidence of this. It was also contended that the provision of faster, modernised services would lead to increased traffic and reduced costs, which would substabtially reduce, if not eliminate the present loss.

The LCGB's tour train of 5 March 1966 pauses for a photo stop near Chilcompton. *Photograph: David Idle; www.transporttreasury.co.uk*

was hauled in both directions by 92220 *Evening Star*. The southbound train – due out of Bath at 3.25pm – was loaded up to 12 coaches; it '…left amidst a salute of exploding detonators and, with the whistle most active, scaled the heights up to Midford in good style'. At Evercreech Junction the train headboard (which, incidentally, has been provided for the last month of running over the S&D) was removed to allow a wreath to be affixed, and then, with nameboard replaced, 92220 continued the last run.

In 1963 it was announced that the S&D was to close on 30 September of that year; the Bath-Mangotsfield line, a crucial connection, was also earmarked for closure. However, the weight of objections was such that the TUCC was unable to deal with them all before the deadline, so there was a reprieve. By this time the services had been run-down to such an extent that there were only four trains from Bath to Bournemouth and three in the opposite direction; all the other services (or what was left or them) were locals – Bath-Templecombe, Templecombe-Bournemouth, and the like. There were, however, the occasional excursions which rekindled memories of 'express' workings. In 1964, for example, there were two Whit Monday excursion trains to Bournemouth West from Bath and Bristol respectively. The Bath train, formed of nine coaches, was headed by 73049 and was piloted by 8F

MINISTRY OF TRANSPORT
St. Christopher House, Southwark Street, LONDON S.E
Telegrams: Transminry, London, Telex
Telephone: WATERLOO 7999, ext.

Our reference RB 3/5/018
Your ref.

18 June, 1965

Dear Miss Hunt,

Somerset and Dorset Railway Closure Proposal

I refer to your letter of 14th April addressed to
Mr. Cohen about the reply of the Somerset County Council
dealing with the bus services for schoolchildren if the
Somerset and Dorset line services are withdrawn.

The Railways Board made an approach to the County
Council on the lines which we suggested to them. The
response has been disappointing as the Board now tell us
that the Council are not prepared to vary their decision
given last year. This was that the Council are unwilling
to accept any responsibility for the "private" scholars
concerned. The Board add they have been told that the
Council's decision has been made with the concurrence of
your Department.

The Board have given us fresh figures of the numbers of
children travelling to Cole from various stations on the
line. The figures show a decrease from the figures given
last year – from 116 to 92. Of these 64 travel on tickets
paid for by the Local Education Authority while the remaining 28 travel on tickets paid for privately. We are trying
to obtain from the Board further information about the
starting points of the 25 children shown as joining the
train at Templecombe.*

Yours sincerely,

Miss D. G. Hunt,
Department of Education
and Science,
Curzon Street,
London,   P. D. Davies
W.1.   This paper is suitable for Dyeline Photocopying

*Now known to
be Templecombe and
immediate district

BRITISH RAILWAYS BOARD   222 Marylebone Road London NW1
F.C.Margetts MBE
                    PERSONAL.   Ambassador 3232

                                 29th June, 1965.

Our ref. T.33-6-17

C.P. Scott-Malden Esq.,
Ministry of Transport,
St. Christopher House,
Southwark Street,
London, S.E. 1.

Dear Peter,

        I know you are aware of our urgent need of decision
on the Somerset and Dorset line case. I can now be a little
more explicit in the reason why this is so important to us.

        The Western Region are aiming to eliminate steam by
the end of this year, but the real stumbling block is on the Somerset
and Dorset line with its steam depots at Bath and Templecombe. If
the decision is delayed much longer, they must either retain steam
for some time or find diesel locomotives and diesel multiple units
for which no provision has been made in their resources. If this were
done it might even be necessary to spend some money on putting the track
into reasonable order to cope with this equipment.

        Anything that can be done to speed the decision will
be a major contribution towards substantial economy.

                        Yours sincerely

P.S. Can we speak
on July 7th?

2-8-0 48660 as far as Evercreech. It stopped
to pick up en route – 40 people were waiting
at Radstock, 70 at Midsomer Norton and
35 at Chilcompton. The train gained 36
minutes on the schedule, completing the
71½ miles in 2 hours 18 minutes which
included nine stops. The Bristol train was
headed by 73051. On the return trips, the
Bath train with 73049 had 76019 attached
as pilot at Evercreech.

In the autumn of 1964 a further cut-
back involved the withdrawal of night
freight services as from 7 September. The
trains affected included the 2.40am Bath-
Bournemouth West mail and 8.12pm
Poole-Bath freight. This enabled the line
to be closed at night – the first time that
had happened since the 1870s. The
nocturnal freight workings were later
referred to in an article in *The Times:* 'All
night long lights burned in isolated signal
boxes like Midford and Binegar and Corfe
Mullen. "There was never time to be
lonely", said the signalman; "you always
had something on the block". At any hour
of the night one might wake to hear the
full-throated exhaust of a heavy freight
pounding its way up to Masbury, with a
sturdy little banker snorting in the rear.
There was the up Poole goods, which
meant that it was high time to turn out
one's bedside lamp; the 2.40am down mail
which had run from time immemorial; and
the "Perisher" which every evening hurried
north from Templecombe up on to the
Midland, steam-hauled to the bitter end'.

The cut-backs of 1964 also included the
gradual withdrawal of the freight facilities
at a number of the intermediate stations,
and the reduction of Midford, Wellow and
Chilcompton to the status of unstaffed
halts.

The S&D had avoided closure, but the
WR was not to be thwarted and, during
1965, the closure plans were dusted off.
Given that the line was again under a death
sentence, the usual two excursions to
Bournemouth on Bank Holiday Monday,
30 August, (worked by 73001 and 73068)
were even better patronised than usual,
many enthusiasts taking the opportunity
to travel on the line while they still could.
The Minister of Transport gave his consent
to the closure and the date was set for 3
January 1966. Once again, though, the sheer
weight of objections – and the fact that
some of the replacement bus services
would not be in place in time – resulted in
closure being postponed for a second time.
This caused the WR some concern, not least
of all because it wanted to completely
eliminate steam haulage that autumn.
Although diesel railcars and multiple-units
were seen at Green Park on services to and
from Bristol, the S&D itself was still
exclusively steam worked. Moreover, to the
best of our knowledge neither Bath nor
Templecombe sheds had had even a sniff
of a diesel shunter; by the mid-1960s there

TEMPLECOMBE PARISH COUNCIL

N. GODDARD
Clerk

15, HILLCREST ROAD

TEMPLECOMBE
SOMERSET

9th August, 1965.

The Rt. Hon. T. Fraser, P.C. M.P.,
Minister of Transport,
St. Christopher House,
Southwark Street,
LONDON, S.E.1.

Sir,

**Somerset and Dorset Railway Line Service
between Bristol, Bath Green Park and Broadstone**

In previous correspondence concerning the above line and the proposals of the Railways Board for closure, the Templecombe Parish Council have stressed that in their opinion little attempt has been made by the Railways Board to introduce methods, and economies, where-by the financial losses may have been reduced. Indeed, we have said that there are indications that there has been a serious attempt to reduce the usefulness of this line by depriving it of traffic, which quite obviously should be routed over this line both from the point of view of economy, and good, and speedy service to the public. In this connection we are now able to give information which confirms our fears and suspicions, and which illustrates the complete lack of honesty of purpose of the Railways Board when considering the usefulness of the Somerset and Dorset line.

Blandford station is a centre for the receipt of large quantities of fertilizer and, prior to June of this year, this freight traffic was being correctly routed via Bristol, and Bath Green Park to Blandford, a service which could be given in approximately four hours, over a route of seventy miles.

Since June of this year this traffic has been re-routed in such a manner as to avoid the use of the Somerset and Dorset line, and we give below details of the method adopted to deprive this line of its usefulness.

On June 13th, 1965, thirty-four wagons of fertilizer (408 tons) left Severn Beach, Severnside siding, Avonmouth, and were routed via Westbury, Salisbury, Eastleigh, and Poole to Blandford. This train required double heading (two engines required) from Poole to Blandford and arrived on June 17th, 1965. (4 days)

On June 20th, 1965 the above was repeated in detail with the exception that the freight arrived Blandford on June 23rd, 1965, thus taking 3 days.

On July 3rd, 1965 34 wagons of fertilizer (408 tons) left Severn Beach, Severnside sidings, Avonmouth and traveled via Westbury, Salisbury, Eastleigh, Poole to Blandford, and arrived on July 7th, 1965. (4 days). This train was worked by a main line deisel engine - and this necessitated the engine of the 07.35 freight train Poole to Blandford having to return to Broadstone to act as Conductor for the driver of the deisel engine, thus delaying shunting operations at Blandford sidings by approximately two hours.

Fertilizer freight trains are also received at Blandford from Haverton Hill, Yorks. Prior to June, 1965 the route has been via Bath Green Park, over the Somerset and Dorset line direct to Blandford, usually a fourteen hour trip, leaving Haverton Hill at 01.40 and arriving at Blandford at 15.30 the same day.

On the 24th June, 1965 a train of 35 wagons (420 tons) left Haverton Hill, York at 01.40 and proceeded via Bristol, Westbury, Salisbury, back to Westbury, and then via Dorchester, Poole, to Blandford, again having to be double headed (two engines) from Poole. This train arrived at Blandford on June 28th, 1965. (4 days)

On July 2nd, 1965, 10 wagons (120 tons) and part of a Block train left Middleton Road, Preston, and arrived at Blandford on July 9th, 1965. (7 days)

It is felt that the foregoing is conclusive evidence that the Somerset and Dorset line is deliberately being starved of the traffic which obviously it should, and could handle more economicaly and expeditously than any other route.

May we again quote from the 1963 Report of the Central Transport Consultative Committee, "....... many objectors still consider that the Railways Board are not interested in improving and modernizing marginal lines, but only in shedding, as quickly as possible, lines which are unprofitable, without first trying to make them pay their way, regardless of the public user. In most cases the public are deeply suspicious of the Board's proposals, and of the facts and figures supporting them."

We maintain that the disquiet that must have been felt by the Central Transport Consultative Committee which prompted them to include such a passage in their report, is fully justified and indeed strengthened by the information we have given. We feel that there is a deliberate attempt by the Railways Board to create adverse circumstances calculated to persuade the Minister to a decision favourable to their proposals for closure.

Furthermore we would observe that not only is this policy of the Board detrimental to the Somerset and Dorset Railway, but to the overall economy of the country, particularly at a time when it is essential that internal services should be handled as speedily, and efficiently, as possible.

Yours faithfully,

[signature]

Clerk to the Council

---

were very few – if any – sheds anywhere in the country that could make that claim.

The last-minute reprieve took the WR unawares, and it had to introduce an emergency timetable for the line. This comprised four trains each way between Bath and Templecombe, five between Templecombe and Bournemouth, and two each way on the Highbridge branch. There were no through trains at all. The S&D might have gained another reprieve, but by this time it was in a dire state. Many staff had already been laid off and maintenance of the stock and the infrastructure had been minimised, so there weren't enough staff or stock to properly operate the few services that were left.

This time, even the most optimistic supporters of the line accepted that closure would come sooner rather than later, so it was unsurprising that many enthusiasts grabbed whatever opportunity they could to visit the line. The Locomotive Club of Great Britain and the Railway Correspondence & Travel Society had already booked special trains for Saturday 1st and Sunday 2nd January, and although the postponement of closure meant that this was no longer the 'last weekend', it was decided to run the trains anyway. Not only were the trains fully booked (the RCTS had to turn away 120 applicants), but the Western Region had announced its intention that steam working would cease as from 3 January and, therefore, any tours after that date could not be guaranteed steam haulage.

The LCGB tour on Saturday 1st started at Waterloo. Merchant Navy 35011 *General Steam Navigation* hauled the train to Bournemouth and continued to Poole and Broadstone, then diverted on to the S&D as far as Templecombe No.2 Junction. At Templecombe, Ivatt 2-6-2Ts 41283 and 41307 took over and

worked the train to Highbridge. From there the train crossed over to the WR main line and 9F 92243 was put on to haul it northwards to Bristol, Mangotsfield and on the Bath Green Park. However, the 9F failed near Warmley, so 8F 48760 had to be summoned from Bath to haul the 9F and the ten-coach train from there to Green Park. The next leg was from Green Park to Templecombe; this was double-headed by 48760 and another 8F, 48309. At Templecombe the train diverted to the SR main line for a direct journey back to Waterloo behind 35011.

The RCTS tour the following day started at Waterloo and, like the LCGB tour the previous day, travelled via Bournemouth to Broadstone. At Broadstone, 34015 *Exmouth* and 'U' class 2-6-0 31639 took over and hauled the train to Bath. 8F 48309 was put on at Bath and took the train via Mangotsield and Bristol to Highbridge, where Ivatt 2-6-2Ts 41283 and 41307 (the same pair that had worked the LCGB special the previous day) took over. The Ivatts worked the train through to Templecombe where Merchant Navy 35011 (again!) was waiting to take it back to Waterloo.

The LCGB special approaches Radstock.
Photograph: John Scrace

The Great Western Society's 'Somerset & Dorset Railtour' of 5 March 1966 was a slightly less glamorous affair than the LCGB tour, being formed of just three coaches and hauled by grubby 8F 48760. The train did a straight run from Bath to Bournemouth Central and back – this is the southbound working passing Binegar. *Photograph: John Scrace*

8F 48706 and Standard Class 4 2-6-4T 80043 head the SLS's rail tour southwards through Templecombe on Sunday 6 March 1966. *Photograph: John Scrace*

The SLS tour of 6 March 1966 included a trip on the Highbridge branch. This part of the tour was worked by Ivatt 2-6-2Ts 41307 and 41249; this is the train waiting at the S&D platform at Templecombe Upper. *Photograph: John Scrace*

Having worked the SLS special of 6 March from Bath to Templecombe Upper, 8F 48706 takes on water. Class 4 2-6-4T 80043 (behind) is presumably waiting to do the same. *Photograph: John Scrace*

The itinerary of the LCGB's 'Dorset & Hants Railtour' of 16 October 1966 included a trip from Broadstone to Blandford Forum and back. This is Class 4 76026 with the Blandford-bound train at Corfe Mullen. Given that there were no turning facilities at Blandford, Class 3 2-6-0 77014 was at the rear of the train so that it could haul the return leg to Broadstone and on to Poole. *Photograph: David Idle; www.transporttreasury.co.uk*

Various reports of 'ordinary' workings on the S&D that weekend appeared in the railway press. For example, on Saturday 1 January (which would have been the 'last day', had closure been effected as planned on Monday 3rd) '…a large crowd of people boarded the 9.50am Bath-Bournemouth. It was hauled by a very disreputable 73001. The train left about five minutes late, comfortably full. Although the engine was in poor external condition and sounded little better, it arrived at Radstock only one minute late; it was on time at Midsomer Norton and arrived punctually at Evercreech Junction at 10.55'. Another report noted that '…the 12.05pm Templecombe-Bath was hauled by 2-6-4T 80041 and the 11.45am Bournemouth-Bath was hauled as usual by Class 4 4-6-0 75072. The 1.16pm Evercreech Jct-Highbridge, consisting of its usual BCK and a van, left behind 41290. It was packed, mainly with enthusiasts. The return trip – the 2.18pm from Highbridge, with 41296 – was jammed tight, passengers standing cheek by jowl in the corridor. It was noted that 'the loco gave a sprightly ride to Templecombe'. The 4.18pm Templecombe-Bath was hauled by 75073.

The S&D's latest reprieve proved to be its last. The problems with the replacement bus services were soon ironed out and closure was re-set for Monday 7 March. The last weekend saw four rail tours. On Saturday 5th the LCGB ran a tour which started at Waterloo, Merchant Navy 35028 *Clan Line* hauling the train directly to

Templecombe. At Templecombe, Ivatt 2-6-2Ts 41249 and 41307 took over and hauled the train to Highbridge and back to Evercreech Junction. From Evercreech, 34006 *Bude* and 34057 *Biggin Hill* took the train on to Bath and then all the way back down the S&D to Bournemouth Central. From there, *Clan Line* took the train back to Waterloo. There having been several photographic stops on the S&D earlier in the day, arrival back at Waterloo was not at the scheduled time of 8.40pm, but at

10.10. The other rail tour that day was a Great Western Society special from Bath to Bournemouth and back. It was worked by 8F 48760 in both directions.

There were two more tours on Sunday 6 March – the very last day of the S&D's existence. The RCTS's 'Somerset & Dorset Farewell' tour started at Waterloo, 35028 *Clan Line* hauling the train to Broadstone and then diverting up the S&D as far as Templecombe No.2 Junction. This is believed to have been only the third time

(it was definitely the last) a Merchant Navy had been on the S&D. Ivatt 2-6-2Ts 41249 and 41283 took over at Templecombe and worked the train to Highbridge. From there, 34013 *Okehampton* took the train via the WR main line to Bristol and thence to Mangotsfield, where 'Hymek' D7014 was put on to the rear and led it on to Green Park. From Bath, 34013 and 34057 *Biggin Hill* took the train to Templecombe, where they handed over to 35028 for the homeward leg to Waterloo. The other special that was organised by the SLS, 8F 48706 and Class 4 2-6-4T 80043 working from Bath to Bournemouth Central and return.

The 'last weekend' specials received considerable publicity in the contemporary railway press – and understandably so – but surprisingly little attention was paid to the last 'ordinary' workings on the line. For the record, though, the last 'ordinary' freight between Bath and Radstock and return on Friday 4th (dep. Bath 3.00pm) was worked by 8F 48760, and on Saturday 5th March the 2.00pm Templecombe-Bath was headed by Ivatt 41307 and Standard 2-6-4T 80138 while the 4.25pm return from Bath to Templecombe was headed by Standard 2-6-4T 80043.

..........oooooo000ooooo..........

The closure of the S&D was reported in *The Times* on 4 March 1966: "'It's curtains for us, I'm afraid," said the signalman, months before the closure of the Somerset & Dorset was officially announced. He had almost wept, when he last travelled up the line to which he had given a lifetime of service, at the peeling and untenanted stations "reduced to unstaffed halts", their prize-winning gardens gone to wild, signal-boxes gutted and sidings ripped out. Together we had watched the running down process, the withdrawal of "The Pines" and the holiday expresses and the excursion traffic, the re-routing of the through freight, the creeping sense of dereliction and decay; once again it had become the Slow and Dirty'.

However, not all of the line had closed completely. A ¾-mile long section at the Bath end was retained for coal traffic to the Co-op siding at Twerton, the section between Writhlington Colliery and Radstock was retained for coal traffic from Writhlington (a new connection to the ex-GWR branch west of Radstock station had been installed so that the coal – which was for Portishead Power Station – could be taken out via Bristol), the section between Highbridge and Bason Bridge was retained for milk traffic from the latter, and the Broadstone-Blandford section remained open for ordinary goods and milk traffic.

As well as the ordinary workings, there were a few specials. One was the LCGB's 'Dorset & Hants Railtour' of 16 October

77014 leads the LCGB railtour of 16 October 1966 on the return leg from Blandford to Poole. This is the train leaving Broadstone. Class 4 2-6-0 76026 is at the rear of the train. *Photograph: David Idle; www.transporttreasury.co.uk*

The Manchester Rail Travel Society's 'Hants & Dorset Branch Flyer' of 25 March 1967 included a trip from Bournemouth Central to Blandford and back to Poole. This leg of the tour was handled by Ivatt 2-6-2T 41320. This is the tour train at Blandford. This tour, incidentally, also took in the Fawley, Lymington and Swanage branches. Not a bad day out! *Photograph: David Idle; www.transporttreasury.co.uk*

1966. The train started at Waterloo and its itinerary included a trip from Broadstone to Blandford. Given that there were no turning facilities at Blandford, the train was top and tailed by Class 4 2-6-0 76026 and Class 3 2-6-0 77014. (76026 led towards Blandford). There was another tour on 25 March 1967 when Ivatt 2-6-2T 41320 hauled a five-coach train on a tour of various branch lines in south Dorset. The tour – organised by the Manchester Rail Travel Society – took in the Broadstone-Blandford section of the S&D. On 15 June 1968 an excursion ran from Blandford to Kew Bridge, calling at the closed stations at Bailey Gate and Broadstone. Part of the special working instructions for the train was that, on the S&D section, passengers entrained or alighted at the disused stations entirely at their own risk. Unfortunately, details of the engine seem to have gone unrecorded. The return train from Waterloo ran only as far as Bournemouth, as trains were allowed to run on the remaining portion of the S&D only during hours of daylight. On 12 May 1973 the RCTS's 'Bristol Avon' Tour – a three-car DMU packed with 160 or so passengers – included a trip over the ex-GWR Frome-Radstock branch and, on arriving at Radstock, the train reversed up to Writhlington Colliery sidings.

...........ooooo0000ooooo.........

The surviving sections of the S&D closed in a piecemeal manner:

30 November 1967: Bath Junction-Bath Co-op Siding (Twerton)

6 January 1969: Blandford-Broadstone

3 October 1972: Bason Bridge-Highbridge (had also been used for construction traffic during the building of the M5 in 1971)

19 November 1973: Writhlington Colliery-Radstock

For the record, the last coal train from Writhlington Colliery ran on Friday 16 November. This was the very last revenue-earning train on S&D metals but, unfortunately, details of the locomotive on this 'landmark' job seem to have gone unrecorded. The pilot duty at Radstock – a Class '08' job – ceased on 5 January 1974.

The MRTS's tour of 25 March 1967 waits to leave Blandford.
Photograph: David Idle; www.transporttreasury.co.uk

The MRTS's special passes Corfe Mullen signal box on its way back from Blandford. *Photograph: David Idle; www.transporttreasury.co.uk*

The MRTS train at Spetisbury. *Photograph: John Scrace*

The photographer had clearly cadged a ride on the footplate of 41320 for part of the Blandford-Poole leg of the MRTS's tour of 25 March 1967. This is the train approaching Broadstone Junction. One assumes that the photographers lined up across the SR main line had confirmed that nothing was due. Otherwise – anyone for ten-pin bowling? *Photograph: David Idle; www.transporttreasury.co.uk*

And finally...

Approaching Masbury Summit for almost the very last time – the LCGB's special of 5 March 1966. *Photograph: David Idle; www.transporttreasury.co.uk*